We Are Adequate To The Task

What twisted path of logic
must our mind walk down
to bring on fear of achieving?
Life has an abundance to offer,
and we are not inadequate to the task.
Innate to our souls is an endless power
to innervate all things around us,
and to possess all good things
through noble endeavor.
A kind and wise God has equipped us
with all that we need to find joy here
and in His world.
We have to think lofty ways
to inspire our life.
We owe Him no less,
for truly, we can say He is our Father
and we, his children.

Wade B. Cook

Business Buy The Bible

Business
Buy
The Bible

Financial Wisdom
Of The Ancients

Wade B. Cook

Lighthouse Publishing Group, Inc.
Seattle, Washington

Library of Congress Catalog-in-Publication Data
Cook, Wade.
Business buy the Bible : financial wisdom of the ancients
Wade B. Cook.
p. cm.
1. Business—Religious aspects—Christianity.   I Title.
HF5388.c66   1997
261.8′5—dc21
ISBN (cloth): 0-910019-68-1

"This publication is designed to provide accurate and authoritative information in regard to the subject matter covered. It is sold with the understanding that the publisher is not engaged in rendering legal, accounting, or other professional services. If legal or expert assistance is required, the services of a competent professional person should be sought."
From a declaration of principles jointly adopted by a committee of the American Bar Association and committee of the Publishers Association.

Book Design by Alison Curtis
Dust Jacket Design by Angela D. Wilson

Lighthouse Publishing Group, Inc.
a subsidiary of Profit Financial Corporation, Inc. (PFNL)
14675 Interurban Avenue South
Seattle, WA 98168-4664
(206) 901-3000
(206) 901-3100: fax
1-800-706-8657
http://www.wadecook.com

10 9 8 7 6 5 4 3 2 1

To John Childers, and his wife, Brenda:
God has blessed our family with your
love and friendship.

Also in memory of my sister, Benita:
A wonderful person, who passed away as a
young mother.

And to her sons, Jay and Eddie:
and Jeannine, Kayli, Stephen, and Taylor, who
carry on and love so much.

Contents

Other Books by Wade B. Cook:

Wall Street Money Machine
Stock Market Miracles
Bear Market Baloney
Wall Street For Real People (Autumn, 1997)

Real Estate Money Machine
Real Estate For Real People
How To Pick Up Foreclosures
101 Ways To Buy Real Estate Without Cash

Blueprints For Success (Summer, 1997)
Wealth 101 (Summer, 1997)
Brilliant Deductions
555 Clean Jokes

$Foreword$

I have been a seminar speaker since 1983. During my first year as a speaker I met Wade Cook. We have been very good friends since that time. I was drawn to Wade because of certain characteristics that he possesses. He knows where he is going and has guidelines that he follows to help keep him on track. I can relate his characteristics to a seminar that I used to teach about the guidelines businesses should follow. I would teach about companies like IBM, which have always been considered top-of-the-line, quality companies, which only subscribe to guidelines which produce the best products money can buy. IBM is known for very high quality products that are expensive.

Wal-Mart, on the other hand, came along and became an unequaled success story in this country. They, however, did not follow the same guidelines as IBM. Their guideline was to give Wal-Mart customers, "good quality at a good price." This seemed to be what the majority of the people wanted. This business guideline was successful for Wal-Mart and became their guiding principle.

I feel that all companies subscribe to their own unique set of guiding principles. These principles determine who they are, what they are and where they are going. I noticed a set of guiding principles in Wade Cook. Because of this, he has become a lifelong friend. His unique guidelines help him keep on track. We all go through periods when circumstances in our jobs, in our careers, in our families or whatever might knock us off of our self-determined track. We usually "react" to these circumstances rather than using our own principles to get us back on our correct path. Wade always seemed to get back on track by sticking to his set of guiding principles.

As I got to know Wade better, I waited to see what his guidelines were that help him stay focused on where he was going. We discussed a simple three-step process. He put God first, put his family second, and put his career third. This model hit home with me because, at that time in my life, I had put my career first, my family second, and certainly God was third. I realized that I needed to follow his guidelines if I wanted to stay focused like Wade was able to.

In the seminar business of 1983, as speakers, we had to do something that we no longer have to do. I credit Wade and his three simple guidelines for this change. Back then, if you wanted to be a seminar speaker on a national level, you had to present your seminars on Sunday. There was not a national speaker that was willing to stick to a set of guidelines regarding this day of the week. Finally, Wade Cook said, "Enough is enough, I will go back to my guiding principles."

He was such a powerful force in the seminar business that when he said that he would no longer speak on Sundays, the promoters took notice and things changed. Now, in this same seminar circuit, no seminars are done on Sunday. I believe that this is due to the fact that Wade Cook changed an entire industry. He made us realize that we need to follow guiding principles. We should put God first, our family second, and our careers third. In the book that Wade has just completed, I find that he shows others how to have guiding principles and how to be tremendously successful in business while sticking to these guiding principles.

John Childers
Author: ***The Lazy Way To Buy Real Estate***
Investor, Financial Lecturer

Preface

The Bible is a collection of revelations, letters, and various fragments from scrolls, all collected and compiled over many centuries. It is indeed the word of God. It shows His dealings with numerous people over millennia.

It is the reading of God's words and then doing them that leads us back to Him. He is so ready to bless us by giving to us understanding of the true and lasting wisdom of His word which will add so much to our lives. I look at people and study their lives. I surely don't see that rich people are any happier because of their riches. I also don't see poor people any happier because of their circumstances.

I do see that the Bible, once its words penetrate the heart and soul of any person, makes them happy. It gives us hope, and it gives us a road to walk on. I truly believe the Bible is for us to live by. I mean to really *live* by. It is a play book—what do we do now? It is an answer book to really tough questions and situations. It is a spiritual guide book.

My small attempt in this book is to cause you to read the Bible more and *buy* into its principles. I know you will be better off. I know your relationships will improve. I know our country and our companies will improve as we draw close to God's word.

My career has been teaching money principles. From real estate to the stock market, from tax strategies to asset protection, I have tried to teach enthusiastically and employ as many of God's principles as possible. This can even be done without blatantly quoting scripture. You see, I think these Godlike principles ring true to people's souls.

Countless people have approached me and shook my hand. Some couldn't even speak because they were so happy to hear these words, these principles, used. They too have wanted to live and use these words in their lives and their businesses. Other times, I would quote directly from the Bible. No one ever left the room. These words have meaning—far beyond my feeble attempts to prove points.

That is the point: the words of the Bible are powerful. They give understanding, they can be trusted and used every day. We don't have to be a Sunday Christian. We can be an Everyday Christian. We can walk uprightly in His covenants all the time.

You will read in this book many wonderful passages from God's prophets. Their words are sharp and powerful, and often cause us to look again at our own lives. They call us to change—they call us to repentance. The words, if we follow them, will lead us back to Him.

I don't think God has a problem with wealth. I think we do. He has everything and He is willing to share all He has. We are the ones who put our hearts in the wrong place. It is you and I who get anxious and toil and spin. He said simply: "Be still, and know that I am God." (Psalms 46:10)

He wants our devotion and our hearts, and then He will work mightily. He loves each one of us way before we come to love Him. I said, "each of us." One way He blesses people is through the efforts of others.

I continually see three major concerns of God. One, love God. Two, obey the commandments. Three, love one another. Jesus spent His life teaching and showing these three things.

This book cannot compare to reading the actual scriptures. All it can do is compile various passages, put them in a topical order, show how they can be used daily and then get out of the way as you, the reader, continue to study them and use them.

You might wonder who I am and what right do I have to write this book? I wonder and think on this all the time. I have collected scriptures dealing with wealth, success, service, et cetera, for years. Seriously, ten years ago, I came up with the idea for this book. I intimidated myself out of writing it. Then, not more than three weeks ago, I said, "It's time." I completed about a chapter a day. I have never had such a passion for anything I've done (and I've written about 20 books).

The scriptures have flowed and I have felt God's hand. I am reverenced and humbled. All I can hope for is this: as you read these pages and ponder the scriptures that I've used, you'll say, "Wow, this is really cool stuff." If these humble attempts of mine cause you to go to the Bible to read more, then my efforts will be a success.

I love my family. I want to be with them. I hope this book lets you be a better parent, or a better child if your parents are still living. I hope you can care more and share more. I hope you can give more time and money to your church and other needs, causes, and people.

I hope this book helps us reconcile our material lives with our spiritual lives. God has abundance for us in both areas. Third John verse 2 says: "Beloved, I wish above all things that thou mayest prosper and be in health, even as thy soul prospereth." I add my prayer to his.

I wrote this preface last. All the chapters were written and almost through typesetting before I wrote this. Although I have done this with my other books, this time is different. While studying the scriptures and writing the chapters I took notes for the preface and concluding chapter. This endeavor was a virtual feast for me. You hang around words like "prosper," "increase," "multiply," "bless," and a host of others, and you grow close to His words. When you see them work, above and beyond all expectations, in your life and the lives of so many around you, then you feel grateful beyond measure.

I hope you have material wealth, but more than that I hope beyond hope that you will be rich towards God. I, like Paul, hope to plant a few seeds, but God surely will give the increase.

Acknowledgments

First, I want to thank God and His love and blessing toward me and my family. He loved me long before I grew to love Him. He blessed me with Laura, my wonderful wife. I love her and my children; Brenda, Carrie, Leslie, Rachel and Benjamin (named after the Son of the Right Hand—Ben Ja Min). I also thank my kind parents, Carl and Helene Cook. They are not only my parents, but my friends.

God has blessed me with friends who have added so much to my life: Tom and Linnet Cloward and their three daughters; Emery, BriAnna and McKell. I love this family like my own; to Jimmie and Patricia Powell and their sons; Jeff and Brian. Nick and Judi Dettman and Warren Chaney have provided powerful insights.

I have had wonderful church leaders who have been true shepherds: Gene Webb, Richard Nielson, Russ Berg, Richard Nichols, Bud Larsen, Earl Ewing, Ralph Matteson (in memory), Eric Marler and his wife Shellie, Ludene Snow and Wayne Snow.

To my staff—loyal and true, my heartfelt thanks: Cheryle Hamilton, Kathleen Mikos, Robert Hondel (watch for his books), Lisa Michaels, Kim and Michelle Brydson, Mark Engelbrecht, Alison Curtis, Angela Wilson, Connie Suehiro, and Judy Burkhalter, and the rest of their staff. Robin Anderson, Margie Huss, Pat Taylor, Jeff Parsons, Ryan Litchfield, Sally and Sean McCarty, Kelly and Steve Heaps, Mike Vogel, Richard Loman, Norman Eade, and so many other leaders and doers on my sales and marketing staff.

My other family members and coworkers: David and Diana Hebert, and David and Debbie McKinlay, thanks for your wonderful attitudes. Other family who have supported me through the years: Dale and Jean Cook, Jeff and Heather Cook, my sister-in-law, Laurie Cook, and Carla Norris, and Jason and Carri Norris, Jerry and Andrea Miller, Shane and Carolyn Norris, and Vaughn and Alaine Tanner.

To my speakers who teach "good stuff" daily: Paul Cook, Steve Wirrick, Dan Wagner, Bob Eldridge, J.J. Childers, Tim Berry, Joel Black, Keven Hart, Pete O'Brien, and Jay Harris.

To longtime friends and business associates: Jeff and Debbie Hochstrasser, Jim and Leslie Landoe, Skip Lindeman, and Paul Johnson.

To my brother-in-law and his wife, Scott and Maria; and to my wonderful parents-in-law, Charles and Sue Scheuerman. I love them as my own.

1

For He satisfieth the longing soul,
and filleth the hungry soul with goodness.
Psalms 107:9

Blessings Unlimited

I need to tell you part of my story. I'm not sure you need to read it, but it is important to me. I hope some of this will be important to you. If you are anxious, if you are too busy, if you have lost balance in life and have wandered from the path, then maybe you'll gain from the following words.

I embarked on my current career in my late twenties. I have not had a paycheck from anyone since I was 23 and got out of the Air Force. I loved to choose my own path. Since I ran my own businesses, I had to make many decisions every day. All the stress of running a business, of traveling, of trying to succeed, was very wearing.

As I look back I can see it. I was so healthy growing up. I had endless energy. For many years I was the one who wore people out. I was in charge and I felt for so many years that everything was up to me.

You know that saying, "If it's to be, it's up to me?" Maybe, but I think it's a half truth. Actually, from God's perspective, it is only true in relationship to the "it" being God's will. This expression, as it relates to success in business, is wrong. It should say, "If it is to be, it is up to God."

7   **The Lord maketh poor, and maketh rich: He bringeth low, and lifteth up.**

1 Samuel 2:7

1

Still, I could not give it up. The business was exciting and fulfilling. In many ways, it still is. But now there is a difference. It's a huge difference. When my heart matured toward God, the results were dramatically better.

A few years ago, I finally quit traveling. I had been gone from home 15 to 18 days a month. Now, I'm gone two to three days and some months I don't travel at all. Now, when I do leave town, it's often for vacations and the kids come with me.

Back then, I would make $25,000 to $75,000 per lecture. This is great money for two to four hours of work. You can see how great the temptation is to travel and speak. Every time I said no, it cost me $50,000. The problem was, I could only be in one city at a time. I believe in what I teach. Thousands of people could use this information. I was tired though, and needed to slow down.

I finally did so. I went cold turkey. Within weeks, we had instructors and facilitators up and running. Within months our business more than doubled. My royalty checks were now much more than before—when I was doing it all.

Being home presented new opportunities and concerns. Within months we were moving into new offices. Our employee count went from 125 to 275. The business was busy. I could work 20 hours a day and never run out of things to do. I became way too busy at home.

We were and are investing in mortgages, hotels, and working our brokerage accounts. We're seeing manifold increases in our business. Each month sees new growth. But, alas, it was consuming me. We climbed to 405 employees.

My good friend, John Childers, called out of inspiration. His long conversation came down to this, "Wade, if you're building a billion dollar company and you are constantly thinking of things which others could be doing and should be doing, you'll never make it." I used to teach this in my real estate seminars. If you paint you get paid as a painter; if you lay carpet, you get paid as a carpet layer. Someone needs to see the big picture—make the deals. This last function is the one which makes hundreds of dollars an hour.

John quoted me out of my seminar. "Wade," he said, "you get paid for what you do!" My wife does this all the time. They use my statements to remind me, or condemn me. I just smiled. I didn't know they were listening.

Back to the point. I know what he said was true but I didn't know how to do it. I wanted a slower, more fulfilling lifestyle, but I was in the fast lane with no exit ramp. I was sanguine after his conversation.

The next morning I left for Hawaii for a six-day vacation with my wife. All I could think of was how to unwind myself from the "busyness." I have so much more I want to do, and when I pray I feel God has so much more for me to do. Humbly, I went to Him in prayer. I knew only He would have the answers.

Was a hundred million dollar public company to be where I stayed? Could I take myself out of the picture and have it still prosper? What else lay in store from me? Are there ways, yet undiscovered, which will let me serve God better? I have only been truly happy when I'm helping others and doing good things. I wanted more chances to serve.

Monday night I arrived home from Hawaii. On the flight home I wrote my first chapter for this book—the one on the ten talents. Please understand I have taught some of these stories and have tried to use scriptural insights in my seminars and workshops for years. I have collected notes and scriptures during all this time. I had put off writing this book for ten years. It was time to stop the procrastinating and get on with it.

All day Tuesday I went from one problem to another at my company. And I saw things that only I, as the founder and owner for many years, would see.

I have half-heartedly joked in the past about my trips to Hawaii. My wife and I love going there. We used to get the hotel room for two weeks. We'd line up the flights. Then we would cut it down to 10 days. Before we left we'd change everything to eight days. We'd get there and come back often in six days and already our business had mutated into something we could barely recognize.

It's nowhere near that bad today. We have great people who are conscientious, dedicated, and loyal. But still, here I was on the day getting back, once again wrapped up in the affairs of the company.

I was worn out by 2:00 P.M. John was in town so we went for a ride. We talked until 10:00 P.M. This was a major discussion. We went around and around. He was trying to get me to focus on the big billion dollar company. I was wondering how to do it. All the theory in the world couldn't answer how I was to conduct my life on Wednesday. It was a great conversation but no hard conclusions — no road map, nor even clear street signs.

This was so frustrating. Why couldn't he and I come up with the answer? He was a lot closer to the solution than I was because he was not only older, but a lot wiser. I'm hardheaded and sometimes need to be hit in the head with a two-by-four to get my attention.

The next morning, I was getting ready to go play basketball. Months earlier, my assistant, Cheryle, gave me a small book entitled *Meditations For Men Who Do Too Much*. It sat unread on my bathroom counter for about six months. I hope you catch the irony here. I was too busy.

It was March 27th. I picked it up and read January 1st. That seemed to be a good place to start. It was one of those books which had a thought, some wise axiom or saying, for each date.

January 1st said, "Let it go." My eyes welled up. I could barely read the following short two paragraphs. I sat there and cried for 25 minutes. No kidding, I just sobbed. I felt relief. I felt like a burden had been lifted from my shoulders.

There was my answer. It was in a book I didn't buy, given to me by a friend concerned about my health, and read after many other in-depth conversations with John and my wife. I know that I have read similar passages in the Bible. My goodness, I have many of them memorized. I know we are not to toil and spin. I know tomorrow will take care of itself. I know all this, but I know it from a mental point of view. I did not buy into it. (Oh, by the way, maybe you can now see why we used BUY in our title: *Business Buy The Bible*.) I know I should have learned these lessons, but I also know one other thing—Paul's admonition is valid:

> 8 **Finally, brethren, whatsoever things are true, whatsoever things are honest, whatsoever things are just, whatsoever things are pure, whatsoever things are lovely, whatsoever things are of good report; if there be any virtue, and if there be any praise, think on these things.**
>
> **Philippians 4:8**

We should seek and find lovely, good, praiseworthy things, and things of good report. It was a marvelous experience that day in my bathroom. I didn't know how I was going to let the business go (at least my intense work in it) but I decided to let that decision go, too. I would strive to walk in more faith. I would let God guide my footsteps.

When I got home from basketball, I thought I would read that day's message, March 27th. Look at what it said: "So now he is a legend when he would have preferred to be a man." I have enjoyed this little book by Jonathon Lazear immensely. I recommend it to you. The publisher is Simon Schuster.

This day's message also had an "add-on" impact on me. Now, I'm not one to put any stock in fortune cookie messages, but this was different. God needed to communicate with me. My prayer, the trip to Hawaii, and especially John's helpful words led me to this point.

Usually I think about new ideas for days before I spring them on my management staff and department heads. That day, I got them all together and discussed my new-found direction. I thought that some of them would be frightened, thinking that their job depended on me. I was so pleasantly surprised with their response. Most came up to me after the meeting and on throughout the day and gave their support. Some received the same peaceful feelings I had.

I can't just walk away from the business, but I can wean myself away—me from it and it from me. I'm President, CEO, and Chairman of the Board of a huge company. I've heard we're the third largest shipper in the state of Washington with one of the major overnight/two-day shipping companies. Microsoft is number one, Nintendo is number two, and Wade Cook Seminars, Inc. is number three. We're big. I have thousands of shareholders who expect the best from me.

I have other paths I must walk. This book is one and this may lead to a whole new purpose/career in life. Will our company become worth one billion dollars? I'm not sure. I think it will. If the new, enabled management team performs and stays true to these great Biblical principles, it will probably happen. I've been going in only two hours a day and already sales are picking up. Once again, as I let go, and try to keep my heart right, we seem to prosper.

This time, freedom has given me the real opportunity to live my passion which is ancient wisdom and teachings. I love old languages. I love links to the past. All I want is, in my humble way, to serve God and do right by Him.

Everything else will take care of itself. Employees will improve their performances. People I don't even know will come on board, bringing a treasure chest of knowledge and experience. Countless thousands of customers will benefit and will be able to do more important things with their lives, if that's important to them.

I wish more than anything I had learned this lesson earlier. I was not ready. I should have made myself ready to be a receptacle for God's spirit. I was a partial receptacle, accepting (screening) what I thought was important. I think most of us are this way.

Total commitment, total giving and total submission is so hard. I think that we evolve and change in a war against who we can truly be. God knows us. He knows where He wants us and what we are capable of achieving. I'm not certain He cares whether we're a butcher, baker, or candlestick maker. I am certain He cares how we conduct our affairs. He wants our heart in the right place. I want to be among those trying to live better.

I have had to learn many of the lessons in this book the hard way. I am hardheaded and usually don't get it. When I do, I'm a dynamo. I'm just saddened by how long it has taken. I hope you can learn from these chapters and implement these principles now so God can start working in your life.

I know I will be criticized for these words. Many people in business and many more in politics want nothing to do with the Bible. It is too hard on them. Some will say that I should teach rehashed, overworked ideas and not keep talking about God and His ways. Some think I should use so many of the fluffy, feel good motivational methods taught by these glitzy, twirling, mental spin-miesters.

Sorry.

This will not be a motivational book, typical or otherwise. It will be motivational to you only if prospering by living the word of God is motivational to you. It is to me. You see, there is just no one I want to go to on this earth to change my personality. I think that should be made to a higher source.

Jesus said we would be criticized (even persecuted) if we choose to follow Him. So be it. I will wear such criticisms as a badge of honor.

Will you end up with a multimillion company or investments? I don't know. Will you enjoy the journey much more? Yes, this I know for sure. Even if you experience hard times and setbacks, you will be on the right road. The right road will lead to true riches. The wealth of this world will help or hinder that process. I'm sure God wants us to succeed.

Fear not, little flock;
for it is your Father's good pleasure
to give you the kingdom.
Luke 12:32

Back To The Ancients

It started with Adam. He had all he needed. In fact, he lived a life of abundance. Nothing was lacking. So, we can literally say that God has provided financial prosperity for those who are obedient to Him from the beginning of time. Adam chose to sin and the results, along with being deprived of spiritual things, produced a loss of abundance. Poverty entered the picture.

This setting is our basis. As we move on to Abraham, we will find many useful statements, lessons, and ideas to help solidify in our hearts and minds God's will towards us. Let's use James as our theme:

> 17 **Every good gift and every perfect gift is from above, and cometh down from the Father of Lights, with whom is no variableness, neither shadow of turning.**
>
> **James 1:17**

The Lord appeared to Abram when he was quite old. We'll list the encounter here:

> 1 **And when Abram was ninety years old and nine, the Lord appeared to Abram, and said unto him, I am the Almighty God; walk before me, and be thou perfect.**

2   And I will make my covenant between me and thee, and will multiply thee exceedingly.

3   And Abram fell on his face: and God talked with him, saying,

4   As for me, behold, my covenant is with thee, and thou shalt be a father of many nations.

5   Neither shall thy name any more be called Abram, but thy name shall be Abraham; for a father of many nations I have made thee.

6   And I will make thee exceedingly fruitful, and I will make nations of thee, and kings shall come out of thee.

7   And I will establish my covenant between me and thee and thy seed after thee in their generations for an everlasting covenant, to be a God unto thee and to thy seed after thee.

8   And I will give unto thee, and to thy seed after thee, the land wherein thou art a stranger, all the land of Canaan, for an everlasting possession; and I will be their God.

9   And God said unto Abraham, Thou shalt keep my covenant therefore, thou, and thy seed after thee in their generations.

Genesis 17:1-9

There is one little word in verses seven and eight that is of particular interest to me. It is the word "and." Look at the use of it the third and fourth time it is used and the second and third time in verse eight and the second time it is used in verse nine. In fact, the Lord uses this word "and" quite frequently in his dealings with Abraham. It is used to include "his seed," or his posterity. His seed is to be included in this awesome covenant and promise.

We can read about this great covenant and see how it applies to Abram, now called Abraham, but is that it? And for how many more generations does the covenant apply to his seed? And even if it extends down through many generations, what does it mean for you and me?

Verses seven and nine say it applies "in their genera-tions." The word is plural. Okay, but are we a part of his seed? Do we qualify if we fulfill our part of this covenant ("walk before me, and be thou perfect" [verse 1], "keep my covenant" [verse 9])?

We need to explore this covenant and in particular, cer-tain aspects of it which deal with prosperity, but let's con-tinue in this qualifying vein to see how we are a part. Why be concerned about its true meaning to us unless we are one of the generations which can be a part of the covenant bless-ing?

Internal to the covenant of Abraham are all of the bless-ings (if obedient) and the curses (if disobedient). God gave it His all. It was complete. He was even willing to give His Son: "He that spared not his own Son, but delivered him up for us all, how shall he not with him also freely give us all things?" (Roman 8:32) The covenant contained all, including Jesus. Jesus could not only fulfill the law, he could make it better. He can make the promises, the greatest which is God being our God, extend beyond this earth. Hebrews 8:6 says: "But now hath he obtained a more excellent ministry, by how much also he is the mediator of a better covenant, which was established upon better promises." This better covenant was brought about "in the blood" of Jesus. Look again at a part, albeit an extensive part, of the covenant as explained in Hebrews:

> 13 **For when God made promise to Abraham, because He could swear by no greater, He sware by Himself,**
> 14 **Saying, Surely blessing I will bless thee, and multiplying I will multiply thee.**
>
> **Hebrews 6:13-14**

(Note that God could not swear by anyone greater than Himself, because He is the greatest. "He sware by Himself.")

32 And we declare unto you glad tidings, how that the promise which was made unto the fathers,

33 God hath fulfilled the same unto us their children, in that he hath raised up Jesus again; as it is also written in the second Psalm, Thou art my Son, this day have I begotten thee.

Acts 13:32-33

God is sure. He fulfilled his promises. Throughout the generations (if the people are obedient and true to His word) His covenant is established.

The last time I asked you to look at verse seven in the seventeenth chapter of Genesis, it was to point out the "ands." It was to show how future generations could participate in this Abrahamic covenant. Now, let's use that same verse to go back to ancient times once again.

"I will establish," are God's words. He did not want someone else to do it. This was a special arrangement: a promise with exceedingly great ramifications.

God seems to deal with his people through covenants: two-way promises. There is something in a covenant for both parties. Here He says, "I will establish," or make sure, make steadfast, put on a firm basis. In the next verse He ends with, "and I will be their God."

Between these two statements, He gives them land. That means a lot. With land they can prosper with flocks, and plants, and also have the security land brings. Even to this day, the people who trace their lineage to Abraham are still fighting over that land. And what happened? Abraham became great, meaning an abundance of riches:

35 And the Lord hath blessed my master greatly, and he is become great: and he hath given

him flocks, and herds, and silver, and gold, and menservants, and maidservants, and camels, and asses.

Genesis 24:35

This was spoken by a servant of Abraham. Later in that same chapter, this servant was sent on a mission and before he left, he questioned: "And I said unto my master, Peradventure the woman will not follow me? (What if she will not follow me?)" He was told to say: "The Lord, before whom I walk, will send his angel with thee, and prosper thy way; and thou shalt take a wife for my son of my kindred, and of my father's house." (Genesis 24:39-40)

In his early days, before the covenant was established, Abraham was blessed. He was following the commandments of the Lord: "And Abram was very rich in cattle, in silver, and in gold." (Genesis 13:2)

Now, let's take a brief look at the covenant working in future generations:

5   **And Abraham gave all that he had unto Isaac.**

Genesis 25:5

(Quick political note: Will all those who tax read this passage? Isaac didn't have to pay an estate or inheritance tax on what his father passed on to him. Please take note and eliminate these taxes.)

11 **And it came to pass after the death of Abraham, that God blessed his son Isaac; and Isaac dwelt by the well Lahai-roi.**

Genesis 25:11

God had said he would continue his covenant with all the seed of Abraham. Let's look at His appearance to Isaac:

24 **And the Lord appeared unto him the same night, and said, I am the God of Abraham thy**

father: fear not, for I am with thee, and will
bless thee, and multiply thy seed for my
servant Abraham's sake.

Genesis 26:24

Wow! Here are the blessings coming to life again. Look
at a few scriptures that we'll list here and explain in other
parts of this book:

12 **Then Isaac sowed in that land, and received
in the same year an hundredfold: and the Lord
blessed him.**
13 **And the man waxed great, and went forward,
and grew until he became very great:** *[Note:
The word "great" here probably could be replaced
with rich. When the word "great" is used, it is usually
followed by a listing of assets.]*
14 **For he had possession of flocks, and possession of herds, and great store of servants: and
the Philistines envied him.**

Genesis 26:12-14

Look, even the Philistines were envious. You see, to them
this wealth translated as might. They asked Isaac to leave:
"And Abimelech said unto Isaac, Go from us; for thou art
much mightier than we." (Genesis 26:16)

Isaac was great, but became very great. He prospered in
fulfillment of God's covenant. Jacob, too, had exceeding
wealth. His father-in-law had dealt unjustly with Jacob for
years. He returned home to Isaac. He had wealth. He com-
mented in Genesis 32:10: "I am not worthy of the least of all
the mercies, and of all the truth, which thou hast shewed
unto thy servant; for with my staff I passed over this Jordan;
and now I am become two bands." He left with a piece of
wood and came back with much wealth.

Jacob prepared a gift for Esau, his estranged brother: two
hundred she goats, and twenty he goats, two hundred ewes,

and twenty rams, thirty milch camels with their calves, forty cows, and ten bulls, twenty she asses, and ten he asses. And even more.

Even in this modern era, this would be quite a gift. In this same chapter, Jacob's name was changed to Israel: "And he said, Thy name shall be called no more Jacob, but Israel: for as a prince hast thou power with God and with men, and hast prevailed." (Genesis 32:38) In that place he also saw God: "And Jacob called the name of the place Peniel: for I have seen God face to face, and my life is preserved." (Genesis 32:30) The covenant God made with Abraham is still alive and well.

Into Egypt

Jacob's son Joseph was sold as a slave into Egypt. Not even a prison could stop the blessings of the covenant. He went from prison to the office of governor. What a promotion! He was set over all Egypt in Genesis 41:42, 44. And what a blessing Joseph became to his father and brothers:

42 **And Pharaoh took off his ring from his hand, and put it upon Joseph's hand, and arrayed him in vestures of fine linen, and put a gold chain about his neck;**

44 **And Pharaoh said unto Joseph, I am Pharaoh, and without thee shall no man lift up his hand or foot in all the land of Egypt.**

Genesis 41:42, 44

Then the children of Israel were enslaved in Egypt:

24 **And God heard their groaning, and God remembered his covenant with Abraham, with Isaac, and with Jacob.**

Exodus 2:24

8   And I am come down to deliver them out of the hand of the Egyptians, and to bring them up out of that land unto a good land and a large, unto a land flowing with milk and honey; unto the place of the Canaanites, and the Hittites, and the Amorites, and the Perizzites, and the Hivites, and the Jebusites.

Exodus 3:8

He remembered His covenant. He once again established it. The people had turned from him and they were enslaved and found in the most wretched of conditions. He sent Moses and the rest is history.

God wanted to meet their need in all ways. He would prosper them if they walked in the covenant. It took years before they were fit once again to have the blessings of the covenant in their lives, but eventually the covenant was restored.

1   These are the words of the covenant, which the Lord commanded Moses to make with the children of Israel in the land of Moab, beside the covenant which he made with them in Horeb.
2   And Moses called unto all Israel, and said unto them, Ye have seen all that the Lord did before your eyes in the land of Egypt unto Pharaoh, and unto all His servants, and unto all His land;
3   The great temptations which thine eyes have seen, the signs, and those great miracles:
4   Yet the Lord hath not given you a heart to perceive, and eyes to see, and ears to hear, unto this day.
5   And I have led you forty years in the wilderness: your clothes are not waxen old upon you, and thy shoe is not waxen old upon thy foot.

6 Ye have not eaten bread, neither have ye drunk wine or strong drink: that ye might know that I am the Lord your God.

7 And when ye came unto this place, Sihon the king of Heshbon, and Og the king of Bashan, came out against us unto battle, and we smote them:

8 And we took their land, and gave it for an inheritance unto the Reubenites, and to the Gadites, and to the half tribe of Manasseh.

9 Keep therefore the words of this covenant, and do them, that ye may prosper in all that ye do.

10 Ye stand this day all of you before the Lord your God; your captains of your tribes, your elders, and your officers, with all the men of Israel,

11 Your little ones, your wives, and thy stranger that is in thy camp, from the hewer of thy wood unto the drawer of thy water:

12 That thou shouldest enter into covenant with the Lord thy God, and into His oath, which the Lord thy God maketh with thee this day:

13 That He may establish thee to day for a people unto Himself, and that He may be unto thee a God, as He hath said unto thee, and as He hath sworn unto thy fathers, to Abraham, to Isaac, and to Jacob.

14 Neither with you only do I make this covenant and this oath;

15 But with him that standeth here with us this day before the Lord our God, and also with him that is not here with us this day:

18 Lest there should be among you man, or woman, or family, or tribe, whose heart turneth away this day from the Lord our God, to go and serve the gods of these nations; lest there should be among you a root that beareth gall and wormwood;

19 And it come to pass, when he heareth the words of this curse, that he bless himself in his heart, saying, I shall have peace, though I walk in the imagination of mine heart, to add drunkenness to thirst:

20 The Lord will not spare him, but then the anger of the Lord and His jealousy shall smoke against that man, and all the curses that are written in this book shall lie upon him, and the Lord shall blot out his name from under heaven.

21 And the Lord shall separate him unto evil out of all the tribes of Israel, according to all the curses of the covenant that are written in this book of the law:

22 So that the generation to come of your children that shall rise up after you, and the stranger that shall come from a far land, shall say, when they see the plagues of that land, and the sicknesses which the Lord hath laid upon it;

23 And that the whole land thereof is brimstone, and salt, and burning, that it is not sown, nor beareth, nor any grass groweth therein, like the overthrow of Sodom, and Gomorrah, Admah, and Zeboim, which the Lord overthrew in His anger, and in His wrath:

24 Even all nations shall say, Wherefore hath the Lord done thus unto this land? what meaneth the heat of this great anger?

25 Then men shall say, Because they have forsaken the covenant of the Lord God of their fathers, which He made with them when He brought them forth out of the land of Egypt:

26 For they went and served other gods, and worshipped them, gods whom they knew not, and whom He had not given unto them:

27 And the anger of the Lord was kindled against this land, to bring upon it all the curses that are written in this book:

28 And the Lord rooted them out of their land in anger, and in wrath, and in great indignation, and cast them into another land, as it is this day.

29 The secret things belong unto the Lord our God: but those things which are revealed belong unto us and to our children for ever, that we may do all the words of this law.

Deuteronomy 29: 1-15, 18-29

So, do these great blessings of wealth (obviously, the spiritual covenants and promises apply to all as God wants all men to repent and come unto him) pertain to you and me? We would have to read outside the scripture to be negative about this. The scriptures do not lie. They point continually to the fact that God wants to be our God, and if we will think of Him first, have faith in Him and His word, and serve Him, we will obtain the blessings of the covenant.

Abraham believed in God. He had faith in his word, but he also was obedient:

5 Because that Abraham obeyed my voice, and kept my charge, my commandments, my statutes, and my laws.

Genesis 26:5

It is the same for us, for our generation. The price has been paid. Now, we must do our part.

The ancient law was given to be a schoolmaster: "Wherefore the law was our schoolmaster to bring us unto Christ, that we might be justified by faith." (Galatians 3:24) In Christ, the new covenant is established for us:"Christ hath redeemed us from the curse of the law, being made a curse for us: for it is written, Cursed is every one that hangeth on a tree. That the blessings of Abraham might come on the Gentiles through Jesus Christ; that we might receive the promise of the spirit through faith." (Galatians 3:13-14)

Note to the reader: The whole 3rd chapter of Galatians is full of inspiring verses: "And if ye be Christ's, then are ye Abraham's seed, and heirs according to the promise." (Galatians 3:29) I suggest you read the entire chapter.

We are heirs. And not only to all that Abraham had promised to him and to us because we are his seed, but also to what Christ has given us. In Romans, it says: "And if children, then heirs; heirs of God, and joint-heirs with Christ; if so be that we suffer with him, that we may be also glorified together." (Romans 8:17) We are one of the "many nations" made of Abraham.

These men of ancient days and men today cannot only be rich, but exceedingly rich. We also do not have to take only a portion. God wants us to have abundance. He wants to bless us "with every good thing." Our side of the covenant requires great faith and good works—walking uprightly as Abraham did.

Summary

The stories and blendings of scriptures from the old and new testaments are my attempt to help all of us learn the blessings of old which still apply to us in our generation. The covenants, blessings, and promises are a wonder indeed. They are to bless us in the here (the old) and in the hereafter (the new). Together, they can make us whole with God and true heirs of His. I'll end this chapter with this final scripture:

9   **Keep therefore the words of this covenant, and do them, that ye may prosper in all that ye do.**

Deuteronomy 29:9

3

And thou say in thine heart,
My power and the might of mine hand
hath gotten me this wealth.
But thou shalt remember the Lord thy God:
for it is He that giveth thee power to get wealth,
that He may establish His covenant which
He sware unto thy fathers, as is this day.
Deuteronomy 8: 17-18

Acquiring Wealth

I love these two scriptures. I particularly like the last part of verse 18, "that he may establish his covenant." It would seem that the power to receive wealth is intrinsic to the covenant. Look again. Could it be that wealth is an integral part of the establishment of the covenant? I challenge you to find one person in the Bible who lacked anything. Yes, you can point to Job (for awhile he lost all), and to Ezekiel, and to a few others who for a brief time had lost all, but these times were temporary and seemed to be used by the Lord to teach or to chastise.

How do we reconcile all this wealth talk with the thought "take no thought," or the injunction "labor not to be rich?" It doesn't seem to be a problem to God. He wants us to prosper. He delights in it. But He also wants our hearts to be set on things of heaven. So, that's the answer. Think of Him first. Think of Him often. Serve Him by serving others. The reward that is everlasting is not of this world.

Are you spiritually ready to prosper materially? Have you considered the covenant? What will you do with abundance? Will it change you? How will it make you better? Are you given to coveting—to thinking of the things of this world? Or are you waiting on the Lord and seeking His Kingdom first? If you are, will you accept what He has to give you?

Back to some of my personal life. I have a beautiful home. I did not seek it. It just came. Look in the chapter on "Eliminating Debt," and then in the "Multiplication" chapter for more on this. I drive a Mercedes because I want quality. I want my home to be of the finest quality. I look at Solomon's Temple, and even the temple where Jesus went—all quality—all made with the finest things the world had to offer.

My heart is not set on these things. I would give them up in a minute. They're nice but they are not worthy of any adoration. They are to enjoy—to find joy therein.

Coveting is not of God. It brings much bad.
Hoarding is not appropriate. See Matthew 6:19-21
Lack is not part of God's plan. His way is to give what we
    need. His way is abundance.

What does He want? He wants His law to be important to us: "Keep my commandments, and live; and my law as the apple of thine eye." (Proverb 7:2) What majestic words. He wants us to have all that He hath, and He is willing—it would even be safe to say eager—to give us all.

However, there is a problem. We have to choose whom we will serve. He says if we serve Him, He will add all these things that we need. Are His statements over thousands of years worthy of trust? I know they are. But, look at this:

24 **No man can serve two masters: for either he will hate the one, and love the other; or else he will hold to the one, and despise the other. Ye cannot serve God and mammon.**

Matthew 6:24

Mammon could be described as idolatry, or worldliness. This scripture is so clear. He doesn't ever say serve one first and then if there's time left over serve the other. He says you'll love one and hate the other. So how does this work? Again, He doesn't want us to think we get wealth by ourselves. Surely it's not that way with salvation. We do all we

can do, but it's up to the Messiah to save us. We are depen-
dent. We cannot save ourselves. It's not God's way. He will
provide for us in all things.

Read again the verse at the beginning of this chapter, "It
is He that giveth thee power to get wealth." Shouldn't we be
walking receptacles? Yes. Should we do our part—trust, believe, obey? Yes, a thousand times, yes. We'll be given ample
opportunity to love others, to care and share; to strengthen,
to console, to cheer, to be a true brother or sister? Everyday
in more ways than we can imagine:

> 2 Set your affection on things above, not on
>   things on the earth.
>
>   Colossians 3:2

How do we then go about our days? We do so by doing
whatever we can do to be "rich toward God." How? One way
is to read the scriptures. They are here to bless us:

> 8 This book of the law shall not depart out of
>   thy mouth; but thou shalt meditate therein
>   day and night, that thou mayest observe to
>   do according to all that is written therein: for
>   then thou shalt make thy way prosperous,
>   and then thou shalt have good success.
>
>   Joshua 1:8

Once again the material and spiritual are linked. Look at
this next verse:

> 2 Beloved, I wish above all things that thou
>   mayest prosper and be in health, even as thy
>   soul prospereth.
>
>   3 John 1:2

I love this stuff. It helps me see so clearly. My course is
laid out. So is yours. Isaiah says:

19 If ye be willing and obedient, ye shall eat the
good of the land.

Isaiah 1:19

I commend you to Deuteronomy, Chapter 28. It is full of
interesting things. The blessings once again depend on our
obedience to his word.

We want happiness and peace. There is one sure way to
get them. Follow him. Why do we want riches? I've asked
this question often. I am very rich by the economic standards of the day. I can truly say it does not bring happiness.
If you do not walk uprightly, if you do not treat God's abundance as a good steward would, then all your wanting just
gives you more wanting. In the end, you'll be left wanting.

"So I can be happy," "So I don't have to worry," "So I can
give my kids things." The answers go on. Once in awhile
people will say, "So I can slow down," "So I can spend more
time with my family," et cetera.

By now, you probably know my answer to all of these
statements. I have used some of these statements myself.
But, where is trust? Where are our priorities? Where can we
go for wisdom and understanding on this? There is probably no better person to turn to than Job.

The same question is asked in Chapter 28. He goes on to
say that man doesn't know the price:

12 But where shall wisdom be found? And where
is the place of understanding?
13 Man knoweth not the price thereof; neither
is it found in the land of the living.

15 It cannot be gotten for gold, neither shall
silver be weighed for the price thereof.

Job 28:12, 13, 15

You see, we can't buy wisdom with gold or silver, or any
other precious jewels. As a matter of history, gold and sil-

ver—riches have caused people to be unwise. They do the very things they shouldn't do to please God. They blow it. How silly to be blessed of God and then turn from Him. God answers Job's questioning in verse 28:

> 28 **And unto man He said, Behold, the fear of the Lord, that is wisdom; and to depart from evil is understanding.**
>
> **Job 28:28**

And lastly, from the Book of Exodus, we run into that word "peculiar" once again. This time it is in a sentence with the word "treasure":

> 5 **Now therefore, if ye will obey my voice indeed, and keep my covenant, then ye shall be a peculiar treasure unto me above all people; for all the earth is mine.**
>
> **Exodus 19:5**

To think that I can be a "peculiar treasure" to God definitely makes me think, "What peculiar things will I do today? How will I make the promises of the covenant alive and active in my life? How will I be a *peculiar treasure*?"

> 2 **Treasures of wickedness profit nothing: but righteousness delivereth from death.**
>
> **Proverbs 10:2**

4

By humility and the fear of the Lord
are riches, and honour, and life.
Proverbs 22:4

Multiplication

God is the ultimate mathematician. He definitely understands addition, but more frequently uses multiplication. Fractions like one-tenth or one-fifth are a part of His calculations.

Numbers fascinate me. I love seeing their relationships. I enjoy the usage of laws—especially the action and reaction; the cause and effects. The use of numbers and simple laws of math are all throughout the Bible.

More importantly for our discussion here, is how these laws of numbers apply and are used by God, and then in return, people's reaction to their usage. Most definitely, His ways are higher—they are so different that I don't think we can understand them unless we really think on them. Once again, our understanding will increase as we see how they work in people's lives.

First, He blesses us with abundance. The abundance of this earth is ours. He provides what we need, usually in ways that encourage us (even enforce us) to acknowledge His hand in all things. Wonderful things are all about us. The delivery methods and results are also wonderful.

Second, He operates through covenants, promises of re-sponsibility with curses and blessings. He blesses those who walk in the covenant.

Third, the results are tangible—they are real.

Fourth, He expects us to use these blessings, this wealth, to further His work. He wants us to serve. Look at Psalms 35:27. He has pleasure in the prosperity of His servant. It doesn't say His rulers, or church leaders (unless they, too, truly serve), but servant:

> 27 **Let them shout for joy, and be glad, that favour my righteous cause: yea, let them say continually, Let the Lord be magnified, which hath pleasure in the prosperity of His servant.**
>
> **Psalm 35:27**

Now, on to the application of these principles. As you read these scriptures notice how often are used words like "abun-dance," "abound," "prosperity," "increase," "full," and "multi-ply."

These are power words. They are used frequently. Almost every time in explaining God's dealings with man, and even in simple story telling these words are used.

Once again, the usage of these words starts with Adam. Genesis:

> 28 **And God blessed them, and God said unto them, Be fruitful, and multiply, and replenish the earth, and subdue it: and have dominion over the fish of the sea, and over the fowl of the air, and over every living thing that moveth upon the earth.**
>
> **Genesis 1:28**

He used the words "multiply" earlier with creatures. Adam was to dress and keep the garden. His seed started to multiply with Seth and Enos and so on. Within a few generations, his posterity was already numerous.

When Noah was to leave the ark, God said:

17 **Bring forth with thee every living thing that is with thee, of all flesh, both of fowl, and of cattle, and of every creeping thing that creepeth upon the earth; that they may breed abundantly in the earth, and be fruitful, and multiply upon the earth.**

Genesis 8:17

The word "multiply" is used with the children of Israel as spoken by Jeremiah. It seems this time the Lord wanted an attitude change—a thankful heart for all He has done. In Jeremiah we read:

19 **And out of them shall proceed thanksgiving and the voice of them that make merry: and I will multiply them, and they shall not be few; and I will also glorify them, and they shall not be small.**

Jeremiah 30:19

I often wonder how God works. I can look about and see the trees and mountains. The stars, moon, and sun are majestic to me. I contemplate the wonder of our human bodies—the complexity of our bodies and how it works stands me in awe.

People inhabit this earth by the billions. Flocks increase, plants grow. When I was younger there was much talk about a population explosion and prediction of famine, or scarcity. Food was to run out, the life as we know it was to end.

But things kept getting better. Technology lets fewer farmers produce more food. New discoveries of oil and gas occur. Whole industries which did not even exist in the 50s and 60s now employ millions. There simply is no credible law of scarcity. We have abundance in this earth. Computer chips from sand, service industries, information and processing ideas, as in the communication arena.

It is the opposite of the predictions. Oh, but those so-called economists get the best sellers, they get the spotlight on TV talk shows. It is simply not God's way. We have renewable resources. We have enough. People teaching financial seminars (or a thousand other seminars) say that there is no free lunch, I look about and see the largest free lunch of all. This whole beautiful earth is a free lunch.

God is our provider. We don't have to be anxious or loaded down. We just need to believe, to work, and to walk uprightly.

He will then do His part, and He will most definitely do it His way. He pointed out much of His way in the latter part of Job. When the test was over, Job received twice what he had before.

I read a quote from a Jewish Rabbi which said, "It was multiplied unto him." Twice is part of the multiplication process so either one will work. To make sure we get it, God lists the amount of animals Job was given:

> 12 **So the Lord blessed the latter end of Job more than his beginning: for he had fourteen thousand sheep, and six thousand camels, and a thousand yoke of oxen, and a thousand she asses.**
>
> Job 42:12

It just seems like the way God does His business. But think of it. Animals multiply and do it exponentially; two becomes four, four becomes eight, then sixteen, thirty-two, and so on. Some do it slower with one offspring per season, some faster with litters of eight or twelve. Some creepy crawly things multiply at an alarming rate—I don't even want to think about it.

If people do it, if animals do it, if birds do it, and if the whole plant kingdom does it, then why can't all forms of wealth grow by multiplication, not addition? And not just any simple sort of multiplication but exponential growth. I see it in nature and now I see it in my bank account, in my business, and in the financial lives of thousands of my students.

Let's look at one hundredfold returns. That's 100 times, or 100x. Isaac farmed. He was righteous and believed in the covenant of his father Abraham:

> 12 **Then Isaac sowed in that land, and received in the same year an hundredfold: and the Lord blessed him.**
>
> **Genesis, 26:12**

After the episode with the young rich man, Jesus's followers were astonished. Who can be saved? Jesus responded that anyone who gives for Him (leaves all if necessary), including leaving family, will receive: "But he shall receive an hundredfold now in this time, houses, and brethren, and sisters, and mothers, and children, and lands, with persecutions; and in the world to come eternal life." (Mark 10:30) They would also receive eternal life in the world to come.

A hundredfold—that's one hundred times. One becomes one hundred. Do we have the faith to sustain us as we wait on the "Lord," and then wait "in this time" to receive what he gives? Some received a 40-fold return, some a 60-fold return, and some a 100-fold return.

Now, please understand what an impact this has had on me. Even before I read this scripture, the process was beginning. Every day I'm humbled by God's blessings. I take my stewardship very seriously. I don't understand it all. I am trying to learn and do God's will for me. I'm not certain that it is different between me and you. We are part of the family of God. But I think because we have different talents and abilities what we are called to do is different. I also think there are more similarities than differences between us.

It is with this in mind I offer the following part of my story. Certain Biblical principles are important to us as we need and use them. I know that this shouldn't be the case, but truly an understanding of God, while at first it comes quickly, it is usually a small understanding, and then it is usually added upon. We grow as we mature spiritually. First the milk, then the meat.

My business is most interesting. I teach people how to grow financially, how to create and protect their wealth. I teach people how to make money. I've always wanted to be a teacher. I thought, as a youth, that one day I would teach college. To do so, to get my degree, I started fixing up old beat up houses. I would think of Bible verses. I had a lot of time to read and listen to tapes.

I found myself wanting to live, I mean to *really* live the teachings in the Bible. I found plenty of opportunities. I would buy, fix up, and sell a home very quickly. Everyone else in real estate was playing the rental game. I tried it but it was not fast enough. I needed income to go back to college. The process was one of serendipity. A friend suggested I sell a home a certain way (where I took back paper—or financed it myself). I did not get cash, but monthly payments or cash flow. I was able to retire in a year and a half on these payments.

I wanted to teach business or whatever; here was my chance. I wrote a book and have been at this career for nigh on two decades. I have tried to incorporate as many principles of the Bible as I can in my investing and in my books.

One principle which has literally made me wealthy was:

10 **And thou shalt not glean thy vineyard, neither shalt thou gather every grape of thy vineyard; thou shalt leave them for the poor and stranger: I am the Lord your God.**

Leviticus 19:10

You see, I would buy, fix up, and then try to sell a house. Sometimes it would take forever to get one sold at market price. Then this scripture entered my life. I won't sell it for the full amount. I'll leave some equity for the next guy. To glean means to go back and get what you missed on the first pass. It means to leave nothing. It is not God's way. His way is to use the bounty of the earth to bless others. A whole business was built around this scripture, the ancient Hebrew law.

Even today I apply it in my stock market seminars and workshops. It is the method behind "rolling stock" and selling before the peak. This principle continues to work. It helps speed up the multiplication process. You won't find it in any financial book, except this one and the Bible. The principle of not gleaning the vineyard has intrinsic to it the promise of blessing others. Don't get greedy. Don't think you have to get every penny out of every deal. Leave something there for others.

When I started my seminars, and though to some people they seemed expensive, I wanted the pricing to be lower than normal. Yes, the company has bills to pay, and huge costs associated with the seminars, but my competitors for similar events in other fields (nothing is similar to my events in this field) and my friends in the business said I could and should sell my course for thousands of dollars higher. And I know we can get it. Our events are sold out everywhere. We have kept the price low. I don't want to take everything—I don't glean the vineyard.

I remembered the meter drop from my taxi driving days: make money on smaller deals. And most of all, I hopefully remember to not glean the vineyard. Once again, this principle works in my life.

Moving On
7   **Be not deceived; God is not mocked: for whatsoever a man soweth, that shall he also reap.**

8   For that he soweth to his flesh shall of the flesh reap corruption; but he that soweth to the Spirit shall of the Spirit reap life everlasting.

9   And let us not be weary in well doing: for in due season we shall reap, if we faint not.

Galatians 6:7-9

I was very successful in my real estate seminars. I loved doing them. My family and I moved back to Washington. I was out speaking for a seminar company and doing very well. I felt that I should go back into business again. I don't know if the running of a business is a blessing or not. I was going to keep it small and absolutely not go into debt.

I started with very little and it blossomed. It grew beyond my wildest dreams — and I have some pretty wild dreams. Let me tell you now what I attribute it to. One day at church a good brother made a promise. We have in my church a fund (offering) for poor people. It is to clothe and feed them. I contribute regularly. Sometimes I want to go to church just to contribute. I see calls for this type of offering or reasons for giving all through the Bible. When I see a poor person on the street corner, and if I'm not sure about him or her, I'll give extra to this fund and let God decide who will get it. This brother said that if we would double our offering we would experience a 5x return in our income. I perked up. This got my attention. He said it with promise and conviction.

Now, I had already gained my own insights into the process of helping the poor. I was successful and didn't just want to be giving of my abundance. I wanted to sacrifice (as the widow's mite) but I was not doing enough. His comments really got me. I interrupted and had him repeat it. I thought I might have heard him wrong. He repeated it and stressed his promise.

I have never made such a promise. I asked, "Let me get this straight. If someone is making $40,000 a year at Boeing and they are paying in, say $50 a month, and now double that $50 to $100, they will have their income increase to $200,000 (five times $40,000 is $200,000)?" "I'm not sure it will come from Boeing, but it will come from somewhere," he replied. "It will have to come from God," I thought. Something else will happen to bring it about.

I looked around the room. Not one other person was interested, at least not outwardly. I said that I teach financial seminars and I make some pretty grandiose claims (in this business you have to back everything up with proof). I teach people how they can double their money, or have a nest egg producing $5,000 to $10,000 a month so they can stay home with their kids. I talk about one week returns, better than most people's annual returns. But I have never made a promise like this good brother did.

Think of this rate of return. I continued, "I don't know about the rest of you, but even if he's only half right, I'm taking him up on it."

Shortly thereafter, my income (take home pay) was over five times as much. We're talking hundreds of thousands of dollars. I doubled it (the offering) again and within a year my take home pay (we teach how to diversify into entities like pension plans, and Charitable Remainder Trusts which allow you to keep more now—or use for good causes now and later) popped up in the millions.

Recently, I wanted to give more but I enjoined God that He need not keep up with the 5x my income growth. Foolish that I am. He'll do what He wants to do. My income, my business has been a real blessing in the lives of others. We teach financial principles based on the Bible (where appropriate). Some principles are just arithmetic and multiplication.

There is no other explanation that I can give. I am far from perfect. I don't even belong in the same sentence as the word perfect. I try every day to find ways to live the truths, the words of God. I earnestly search for ways to use the scriptures in my decision making, my attitude, and all my dealings. I have been so successful that from time to time, I'm criticized for the claims I make.

Wade Cook says you can double your money every 2½ to 4 months, the Bible talks in terms of 100-fold returns. Let's compare. Take $1,000 the Wade Cook way and in three months you have $2,000. In another three months, it's $4,000. Then $8,000, and at the end of the year, perhaps more. You figure it out. Now, not all of your money will do this and the more you have the more effort it takes.

Countless people have turned $10,000 into $30,000; or $20,000 into $300,000. Our files are full of such testimonials. But to take $1,000 and turn it into $100,000 is of the Bible. So, to my students—keep going. Make these principles come alive. To my naysayers—go to the Bible: "Go to the ant, thou sluggard; consider her ways, and be wise." (Proverbs 6:6)

The law of multiplication is alive and well. God's ways are higher—I like His ways. These laws will serve us well if we serve Him well. If we are blessed and in turn bless others, then our blessing will be the eternal.

5 *Treasures of wickedness profit nothing: but righteousness delivereth from death.*
Proverbs 10:2

Get A "Job"

Job's life, as told in the Book of Job, is worthy of exploration. Many principles of wealth, happiness, dedication, and stewardship are contained in this book. This is a thought-provoking story. The story of Job is told passionately and it produces many emotions in us.

He had it all. The Bible says: "There was a man in the land of Uz, whose name was Job; and that man was perfect and upright, and one that feared God, and eschewed evil." (Job 1:1) In many other parts of this book I have read similar words. He was walking in the covenant of Abraham. He was rich by any standard: "His substance also was seven thousand sheep, and three thousand camels, and five hundred yoke of oxen, and five hundred she asses, and a very great household, so that this man was the greatest of all the men of the east." (Job 1:3) He worried about his children; he prayed and offered sacrifices for them. He loved God.

Then a conversation between God and Satan starts. Satan says Job is this way because God had done all these things for him. By the way, God doesn't deny it. God did bless the work of his hand. Job had increase:

8 **And the Lord said unto Satan, Hast thou considered my servant Job, that there is none**

like him in the earth, a perfect and an upright man, one that feareth God, and escheweth evil?

9   Then Satan answered the Lord, and said, Doth Job fear God for nought?

10   Hast not thou made an hedge about him, and about his house, and about all that he hath on every side? thou hast blessed the work of his hands, and his substance is increased in the land.

11   But put forth thine hand now, and touch all that he hath, and he will curse thee to thy face.

12   And the Lord said unto Satan, Behold, all that he hath is in thy power; only upon himself put not forth thine hand. So Satan went forth from the presence of the Lord.

Job 1:8-12

Satan challenged God by saying if Job did not have these things, he would curse God (verse 11). God allowed Satan to enter, "Behold, all that he hath is in thy power." (verse 12)

Notice also that God won't let Satan have any power ("put forth not thy hand") on Job directly. He only had a direct affect on Job's possessions. It is truly an interesting and dramatic challenge. Would Job curse God if he lost everything?

Shortly thereafter, all was lost. His flocks were killed or stolen. Look at Job's response:

20   Then Job arose, and rent his mantle, and shaved his head, and fell down upon the ground, and worshipped,

21   And said, Naked came I out of my mother's womb, and naked shall I return thither: the Lord gave, and the Lord hath taken away; blessed be the name of the Lord.

22   In all this Job sinned not, nor charged God foolishly.

Job 1:20-22

He was steadfast. In chapter two, the plot thickens. The conversation goes on. This time when speaking of Job: "And the Lord said unto Satan, Hast thou considered my servant Job, that there is none like him in the earth, a perfect and an upright man, one that feareth God, and escheweth evil? " and the Lord adds, "and still he holdeth fast his integrity, although thou movedst me against him, to destroy him without cause." (Job 2:3) A wonderful statement. Satan is allowed now to touch his flesh. He just could not kill him (verse 6):

4   And Satan answered the Lord, and said, Skin for skin, yea, all that a man hath will he give for his life.

5   But put forth thine hand now, and touch his bone and his flesh, and he will curse thee to thy face.

6   And the Lord said unto Satan, Behold, he is in thine hand; but save his life.

7   So went Satan forth from the presence of the Lord, and smote Job with sore boils from the sole of his foot unto his crown.

8   And he took him a potsherd to scrape himself withal; and he sat down among the ashes.

9   Then said his wife unto him, Dost thou still retain thine integrity? curse God, and die.

10 But he said unto her, Thou speakest as one of the foolish women speaketh. What? shall we receive good at the hand of God, and shall we not receive evil? In all this did not Job sin with his lips.

11 Now when Job's three friends heard of all this evil that was come upon him, they came every one from his own place; Eliphaz the Temanite, and Bildad the Shuhite, and Zophar the Naamathite: for they had made an appointment together to come to mourn with him and to comfort him.

12 And when they lifted up their eyes afar off, and knew him not, they lifted up their voice,

and wept; and they rent every one his mantle, and sprinkled dust upon their heads toward heaven.

13 So they sat down with him upon the ground seven days and seven nights, and none spake a word unto him: for they saw that his grief was very great.

Job 2:4-13

Next his three friends came. At first, they couldn't even recognize him. They wept and sat with him for seven days. Chapter 3 is Job lamenting everything, but not God. He stayed on course.

We get a good feel for the disaster of Job by statements of these friends who knew him. They probably observed him for years. He helped and was a true friend to people. Look at this:

3 Behold, thou hast instructed many, and thou hast strengthened the weak hands.

4 Thy words have upholden him that was falling, and thou hast strengthened the feeble knees.

Job 4:3-4

Throughout the next several chapters his friends try to give council. Job responds. By chapter 10, he is weary. He wants to be acquitted as he has not sinned. He wants to know why God is punishing him. He feels he is not wicked. He is frustrated:

7 Thou knowest that I am not wicked; and there is none that can deliver out of thine hand.

8 Thine hands have made me and fashioned me together round about; yet thou dost destroy me.

9 Remember, I beseech thee, that thou hast made me as the clay; and wilt thou bring me into dust again?

10 Hast thou not poured me out as milk, and curdled me like cheese?

11 Thou hast clothed me with skin and flesh, and hast fenced me with bones and sinews.

12 Thou hast granted me life and favour, and thy visitation hath preserved my spirit.

13 And these things hast thou hid in thine heart: I know that this is with thee.

14 If I sin, then thou markest me, and thou wilt not acquit me from mine iniquity.

15 If I be wicked, woe unto me; and if I be righteous, yet will I not lift up my head. I am full of confusion; therefore see thou mine affliction.

Job 10:7-15

His friends get a bit self righteous. In verse 3 of chapter 12, he says: "But I have understanding as well as you; I am not inferior to you: yea, who knoweth not such things as these?" He's angry with them and in verse 4 of chapter 13, he lets them have it:

4 But ye are forgers of lies, ye are all physicians of no value.

5 O that ye would altogether hold your peace! And it should be your wisdom.

Job 13:4, 5

The friends attack harder. In my financial seminars, I hope to get people thinking about to whom they are going to go for advice. If you want to make over one hundred thousand dollars a year, why are you talking to anyone (about making money) who is making under $100,000 a year? One of the first things people must do is seek advice (wisdom) from people who are already there. Million dollar ideas are shot down by friends back home making less that $40,000 a year.

Look at the rationale Job's friends use on why he should listen to them in Job 15:10: "With us are both the gray-headed and very aged men, much elder than thy father." So what? Gray hair does not absolutely mean that wisdom abides with that person.

Now Job turns the table on them. Chapter 16:2: "I have heard many such things: miserable comforters are ye all." Job helped people. He was a blessing to them.

His friends are dumping on him. He wants them to know how he would treat them if the roles were reversed. He wants to know why his friends "vex" him, and reproach him ten times. He is not angry with God, but with them:

4   **I also could speak as ye do: if your soul were in my soul's stead, I could heap up words against you, and shake mine head at you.**

5   **But I would strengthen you with my mouth, and the moving of my lips should assuage your grief.**

6   **Though I speak, my grief is not asswaged: and though I forbear, what am I eased?**

7   **But now he hath made me weary: thou hast made desolate all my company.**

8   **And thou hast filled me with wrinkles.**

Job 16:4-8

They seem to be set in their thoughts, that all these bad things are happening to Job because of his sins. Look at chapter 20:4-5, Job 21:27-34, and Job 23:10-11:

4   **Knowest thou not this of old, since man was placed upon earth,**

5   **That the triumphing of the wicked is short, and the joy of the hypocrite but for a moment?**

Job 20:4-5

Read Job's response:

27   **Behold, I know your thoughts, and the devices which ye wrongfully imagine against me.**

28 For ye say, Where is the house of the prince? and where are the dwelling places of the wicked?

29 Have ye not asked them that go by the way? and do ye not know their tokens,

30 That the wicked is reserved to the day of destruction? they shall be brought forth to the day of wrath.

31 Who shall declare his way to his face? And who shall repay him what he hath done?

32 Yet shall he be brought to the grave, and shall remain in the tomb.

33 The clods of the valley shall be sweet unto him, and every man shall draw after him, as there are innumerable before him.

34 How then comfort ye me in vain, seeing in your answers there remaineth falsehood?

Job 21:27-34

10 But He knoweth the way that I take: when He hath tried me, I shall come forth as gold.

11 My foot hath held His steps, His way have I kept, and not declined.

Job 23:10-11

His wondering continues. In chapter 29, he states: "Oh that I were as in months past, as in the days when God preserved me," (verse 2). In the 29th chapter, he lists the things he did before all this bad happened:

12 Because I delivered the poor that cried, and the fatherless, and him that had none to help him.

13 The blessing of him that was ready to perish came upon me: and I caused the widow's heart to sing for joy.

14 I put on righteousness, and it clothed me: my judgement was a robe and a diadem.

15 I was eyes to the blind, and feet was I to the lame.

16 I was a father to the poor: and the cause which I knew not I searched out.

Job 29:12-16

25 I chose out their way, and sat chief, and dwelt as a king in the army, as one that comforteth the mourners.

Job 29:25

Job wants God to know of his integrity. He wants to know what is happening. Chapter 31:6: "Let me be weighed in an even balance that God may know mine integrity." He also wants God to know that he did not put confidence in wealth: "If I have made gold my hope, or have said to the fine gold, Thou art my confidence; If I rejoice because my wealth was great, and because mine hand had gotten much." (Job 31:24-25). His confidence was in God.

Job also:

- Did not curse those who hated him:

30 **Neither have I suffered my mouth to sin by wishing a curse to his soul.**

Job 31:30

- Opened his doors to the traveller:

32 **The stranger did not lodge in the street: but I opened my doors to the traveller.**

Job 31:32

- Paid for what he ate:

39 **If I have eaten the fruits thereof without money, or have caused the owners thereof to lose their life.**

40 Let thistles grow instead of wheat, and cockle instead of barley. The words of Job are ended.

Job 31:39-40

Job was righteous in his own eyes. Well, he was in my eyes, too. He was bewildered and even though he did not curse God, he definitely was trying to justify himself and states that he did not deserve this treatment. His three friends were basically chastising him for being self-righteous.

Another friend, one much younger than the other three, Elihu (the translation of this name means "God is us") waited and then spoke up. He acknowledged the age of all the others but then lit into the three and also into Job. Let's pick it up in Job:

1 So these three men ceased to answer Job, because he was righteous in his own eyes.

2 Then was kindled the wrath of Elihu the son of Barachel the Buzite, of the kindred of Ram: against Job was his wrath kindled, because he justified himself rather than God.

3 Also against his three friends was his rath kindled, because they had found no answer, and yet had condemned Job.

4 Now Elihu had waited till Job had spoken, because they were elder than he.

5 When Elihu saw that there was no answer in the mouth of these three men, then his wrath was kindled.

6 And Elihu the son of Barachel the Buzite answered and said, I am young, and ye are very old; wherefore I was afraid, and durst not show you mine opinion.

7 I said, Days should speak, and multitude of years should teach wisdom.

8 But there is a spirit in man: and the inspiration of the Almighty giveth them understanding.

9   Great men are not always wise: neither do the aged understand judgment.

10 Therefore I said, Hearken to me; I also will show mine opinion.

11 Behold, I waited for your words; I gave ear to your reasons, whilst ye searched out what to say.

12 Yea, I attended unto you, and, behold, there was none of you that convinced Job, or that answered his words:

13 Lest ye should say, We have found out wisdom: God thrusteth him down, not man.

14 Now he hath not directed his words against me: neither will I answer him with your speeches.

15 They were amazed, they answered no more: they left off speaking.

16 When I had waited, (for they spake not, but stood still, and answered no more;)

17 I said, I will answer also my part, I also will shew mine opinion.

18 For I am full of matter, the spirit within me constraineth me.

19 Behold, my belly is as wine which hath no vent; it is ready to burst like new bottles.

Job 32:1-19

There is an interesting and personal side note to his words as he continues in verse 21: "Let me not, I pray you, accept any man's person, neither let me give flattering titles unto man."

As I said, this story is personal to me. You see I have no degrees (actually, I have an Associate of Arts, a two-year degree from a junior college); I have no initials to put after my name.

I'm a guy who has learned how to make a lot of money. God has blessed me with a talent and ability to share this information. For over 17 years, I have taught real estate investment seminars. My real estate books (and now my stock market books) have been in the bookstores for years.

I have taught hundreds of thousands of people and have sold countless books, but still I have no formal training. I've jokingly stated that my one hope is that when we get to heaven there will be no initials after our names.

I've had some seminar promoters insist on listing my credentials in the programs, or on the announcement posters outside the speaking rooms. I would say Wade B. Cook, CD. The CD stood for Cab Driver. It was okay though, because I had initials—I had credentials. These words of Elihu are music to my ears.

Elihu reminds Job of his words: "I am clean without transgression, I am innocent; neither is there iniquity in me." (Job 33:9) He goes on: "Behold, in this thou art not just: I will answer thee, that God is greater than man." (Job 33:12) Elihu goes on for two more chapters with similar statements and calling Job to hear his words.

In chapter 36:2: "Suffer me a little, and I will shew thee that I have yet to speak on God's behalf." Then, without warning, the Lord begins speaking to Job. The Lord, through a series of questions, puts Job in his place: "Where wast thou when I laid the foundations of the earth? declare, if thou has understanding." (38:4), and then in Job 38 and 39 he continues.

Job is humbled: "Then Job answered the Lord, and said, Behold, I am vile; what shall I answer thee? I will lay mine hand upon my mouth." (Job 40:3-4)

The Lord spends one more chapter pointing out what He can do compared to Job. Job is definitely humbled:

2   I know that thou canst do every thing, and
    that no thought can be withholden from thee.

3   Who is he that hideth counsel without
     knowledge? Therefore have I uttered that I
     understood not; things too wonderful for me,
     which I knew not.

4   Hear, I beseech thee, and I will speak: I will
     demand of thee, and declare thou unto me.

5   I have heard of thee by the hearing of the ear:
     but now mine eye seeth thee.

6   Wherefore I abhor myself, and repent in dust
     and ashes.

Job 42:2-6

In the next few verses, the Lord really gets on the three
friends of Job: "And it was so, that after the Lord had spoken
these words unto Job, the Lord said to Eliphaz the Temanite,
My wrath is kindled against thee, and against thy two friends:
for ye have not spoken of me the thing that is right, as my
servant Job hath." (Job 42:7) I love how God keeps calling Job
his servant. Job was to make an offering for them and they
would be accepted because of Job. And now to the finale. The
end is better than the beginning. I am wrapped up in Job's
life. I have felt deeply for him. He lived 140 years after this
experience. I wonder how he feels now that he endured well,
repented when necessary. I believe he would have lived this
long anyway, but how much more fulfilling, how much better able to relate to other less fortunate than he, for having
had these exceptionally harsh experiences:

10   And the Lord turned the captivity of Job, when
     he prayed for his friends: also the Lord gave
     Job twice as much as he had before.

Job 42:10

I wrote about the word "twice" in the chapter on multiplication. For now, look what he was given. Flocks of a huge
number. His was to have friends and family once again. They
honored him:

12   So the Lord blessed the latter end of Job more
     than his beginning: for he had fourteen

thousand sheep, and six thousand camels, and a thousand yoke of oxen, and a thousand she asses.

13 He had also seven sons and three daughters.

14 And he called the name of the first, Jemima; and the name of the second, Kezia; and the name of the third, Kerenhappuch.

15 And in all the land were no women found so fair as the daughters of Job: and their father gave them inheritance among their brethren.

16 After this lived Job an hundred and forty years, and saw his sons, and his sons' sons, even four generations.

17 So Job died, being old and full of days.

Job 42:12-17

At all times, and in all ways we should trust God. Believing on Him, and doing His works will bring true lasting joy.

6

The earth is the Lord's,
and the fulness thereof;
the world, and they that dwell therein.
Psalms 24:1

There Is A Free Lunch

For thousands of years, men set out to create or make gold. It was an alchemist's dream. Thousands of various mixtures and processes have been tried. Gold, for centuries, even millennia, has been a store of wealth, a medium of exchange. It continues to be so today. The commercial uses of gold from industrial use to jewelry, from printing and art to dentistry are legion.

Isn't it ironic that men have so diligently tried to find a way to make gold, but if successful (while helpful) it would drive the price down? Their new-found riches would dissipate under the avalanche of an abundant gold supply. Part of the reason gold is so valuable is because of the difficulty of finding, mining, and processing it to a usable point.

Is the endeavor worth it? I am one who believes in, and lives by, a serendipity philosophy. The many happy and joyous discoveries I've made while looking for, or attempting something has made my life not only interesting, but enjoyable and fulfilling. Likewise, all alchemists' attempts have not been in vain. Some have spurred our pharmaceutical industry. Some have given us more durable metals like steel and aluminum. Others have helped us harvest bigger and better crops.

Truly, we do not live in a world of scarcity, but of abundance. Fewer farms produce enough food in America alone to feed numerous nations. We thought oil, coal, and other resources were depleted, only to find more and develop better extraction processes to make previously unheard of processes now effective and useful.

The miniaturization of machinery and electronics has been the genesis of countless advances in biotechnology, chemistry, communication, information processing, et cetera. Whole industries, employing millions were not even in existence 20 years ago.

You would have to be blind to the facts, naive, or have some idiotic "the sky is falling" book for sale to believe in this scarcity nonsense. Man can make things look ugly for awhile, but we cannot destroy what God has created.

We can make it better. I'm reminded of the farmer, who upon being told how blessed of God he was to have such a beautiful farm, remarked, "You should have seen it when God had it by Himself." Isn't this what God told Adam to do, "to dress it and keep it?"

So, we should make it better. We can clean up our messes, and try not to make a mess or destroy anything if we can help it. The simplest of things, added up, make big differences.

Part of the problem today is that our abundance causes people to forget God. We should be careful and never cease acknowledging His hand in all things. Remember, God cares about everything. We may forget Him, but He never forgets us.

Recently, I was teaching a stock market class. I was talking about rates of returns. Specifically, how you get a better return on smaller amounts of money. One reason is that it's hard to manage larger sums of money. Then I got off the path and said some interesting things. Here is the gist of the seminar:

When you have a lot of money, you start doing stupid things. I used to teach this extensively in my real estate seminars, "Cash talks, but the lack of it generates creativity." "Solve problems with your mind not your cash," I'd say.

Now, here I was, off the beaten path, so I stayed there. I asked the class, "You know the scripture about how hard it is for a rich man to get into Heaven?"

"Something about a camel," they chuckled.

I continued, "You know, I think God wants to be around smart people—people who choose His ways. If rich people do stupid things, then they won't make it." It was done in jest, but when the class was over, I thought that I had once again, inadvertently walked into a truth.

Riches can cause you to act differently. They shouldn't. Riches should increase your ability to do good things. What does abundance do? I've taught for many years that wealth will make you go along the road you've already been on—a little faster. If you're a bad person, it will make you worse. If you're a good person, it will make you better.

I've asked people in my cash flow seminars the following question, "If you had a little extra cash coming in, say even $500 a month, could you be a better you?" I hope people meant, when they nodded their heads, the affirmative. $500, or $5,000, or even $50,000 a month can do wonderful things; piano and gymnastic lessons for the kids, new clothes for your sister, dental work for Uncle Bill, and a better retirement for Grandma. I honestly believe that God blesses us with wealth, not so much for ourselves, but to see how we'll use it for the benefit of others:

> 35 For I was an hungred and ye gave me meat; I was thirsty and ye gave me drink; I was a stranger and ye took me in:
> 36 Naked, and ye clothed me: I was sick, and ye visited me: I was in prison, and ye came unto me.
>
> Matthew 25:35-36

Every day presents us with wonderful opportunities to be a blessing in the lives of others, both with our time, with our money, with our ability to make a difference with all that we can. For most of us, these actions will be small, but think of what they mean to others. Each of us has a treasure chest of wealth: patience, a forgiving heart, hugs, a sympathetic ear, a kind word, a soft-spoken prayer, a gracious heart, a firm and friendly handshake, and many more. It doesn't just take money to help others or make them happy. Where is our heart and what decisions must we make to strengthen our resolve to make better choices? It is this resolve that will carry us through.

Jesus did not condemn wealth. He told stories of it frequently. He was the one who said to take the unused talents from one and give to another. He allowed costly ointment to be administered to His feet. He is the one who made it so we can finally, after all we do, be joint heirs with Him and receive all that the Father has. He also allowed Zacchaeus to keep part of his ill-gotten gains without condemning him. Many hoped that the Messiah would come to rule the country (earth), kick out the Romans and be their king. He, by His word and actions, came and wanted to be King of our souls, our spirits. He wants our hearts to be in the right place. Let's review the story of a rich young ruler asking Jesus what he must do to inherit eternal life:

> 18　And a certain ruler asked him, saying, Good Master, what shall I do to inherit eternal life?
>
> 19　And Jesus said unto him, Why callest thou me good? None is good, save one, that is, God.
>
> 20　Thou knowest the commandments, Do not commit adultery, Do not kill, Do not steal, Do not bear false witness, Honour thy father and thy mother.
>
> 21　And he said, All these have I kept from my youth up.
>
> 22　Now when Jesus heard these things, He said unto him, Yet lackest thou one thing: sell all

that thou hast, and distribute unto the poor, and thou shalt have treasure in heaven: and come, follow me.

23 And when he heard this, he was very sorrowful: for he was very rich.

24 And when Jesus saw that he was very sorrowful, he said, How hardly shall they that have riches enter into the kingdom of God!

25 For it is easier for a camel to go through a needle's eye, than for a rich man to enter into the kingdom of God.

26 And they that heard it said, Who then can be saved?

27 And he said, The things which are impossible with men are possible with God.

28 Then Peter said, Lo, we have left all, and followed thee.

29 And he said unto them, Verily I say unto you, There is no man that hath left house, or parents, or brethren, or wife, or children, for the kingdom of God's sake,

30 Who shall not receive manifold more in this present time, and in the world to come life everlasting.

Luke 18:18-30

There are parallel accounts in Matthew and Mark. This man was a good man. The law was important to him. I think Jesus really liked this guy. But wealth created a problem for him and Jesus was asking him to declare his allegiance. He went away sorrowful "for he was very rich."

You don't see Jesus condemning him. Maybe the ruler followed later. Maybe he hadn't had time to develop spiritually to have the faith necessary to give "nothing wavering." To me, this set of scriptures, this story, just points out that wealth creates a problem. A problem of where your heart, your allegiance, truly lies: "But let him ask in faith, nothing wavering. For he that wavereth is like a wave of the sea driven with the wind and tossed." (James 1:6)

And again, two masters cannot be served. We must choose God first. And now, I'll ask the question of all questions: if we do not choose God first, does any other choice really make a difference?

As my wife says, "every choice we make makes a difference—either toward God or away from God." We can learn from this young rich man. Review the Abrahamic covenant: Job being faithful and receiving twice as much as before, the statements made in Mark, and those in the story of Isaac, about "100-fold."

One Hundred-Fold

God stands ready to bless us. He is knocking at the door. Are we ready to let Him in to bless us spiritually first, then materially? I think most people are not ready "mentally or spiritually" for all that He has to give us.

> 9 But as it is written, Eye hath not seen, nor ear heard, neither have entered into the heart of man, the things which God hath prepared for them that love him.

1 Corinthians 2:9

(Note: Verses 10 through 16 in this same chapter are also very instructive. I suggest you study them.)

This, to me, is the main point—making sure we give credit where credit is due, or making sure our heart and thoughts are in the right place. I can't find anywhere where God says it is a sin to be rich. Likewise, I can't find one reference to justify a thought that to be poor is a sin. There are many references to doing the right things. Even slaves were told to serve well. Whether a slave, a bondman, a ruler, a merchant, a fisherman, or a tax collector, it is the same—purify your hearts, serve Him by loving one another.

You see, being rich is relative anyway. Take Solomon for example. He was wise and served God. He had built an awesome temple. The workmanship was exceedingly fine. The best stone, jewels, wood and ornaments were used. It took years to build. Imagine putting next to it a small, ruggedly built house—by today's standards a poor person's house, with electricity and indoor plumbing, with an old beat up refrigerator, a TV without remote control, a toilet with the seat half attached, a furnace which doesn't work too well, and only a window air conditioning unit.

Which one do you think Solomon would choose? Would he give up the majestic courts, the impressive hallways, the beautiful gardens—indeed would he give up the throne to spend one winter night in a warm room with a bed, or one hot afternoon in an air-conditioned room with his favorite Psalm of David musical score on his boom box? We would think this poor person's circumstances are awful or at least a little sad. People of Solomon's time, or Jesus's time, would think this person rich beyond measure.

My personal blessings have far exceeded what I would have dreamed for. I make millions, and yet I can imagine some really rich person saying, "You know Harold, those days were sure fun, back when we were only making $200,000 a month." To them, I am poor financially. Is wealth relative? Yes, and we need to keep this in perspective. We need to make sure our richest of riches is God's kingdom. We serve Him first, and all else will be added.

One of the biggest thrills of my life was to build a nice house for my wife's parents on our property. Her mother helped with the plans—so she can have a home which suits her. Her father was excited. We have a beautiful, peaceful property. We have here many things they enjoy doing.

Personally, I'm doing this so my wife and her parents can spend more time together, and so our kids can be around their grandparents. My parents live 50 minutes away and the wealth given me allowed me to buy them a home. Recently, my dad needed a new hearing aid. We paid cash for it—no financing, which my father is so accustomed to. He has financed nearly everything in his life. The credit union is one of his favorite places to go. He's on a first name basis with many there.

I'm not writing any of this except to acknowledge God's hand and express my gratefulness for His abundance towards us. I think of Job, Abraham, Isaac, and many others. They lived right. They walked in God's covenant. Think of the hundreds, possibly thousands of people in their families and their households. You probably have heard the expression, "the tide rises all boats—both big and small." The number of Abraham's household were directly blessed because of the abundance Abraham enjoyed.

You are associated with many people right now. Are you really a part of their lives? We are all so very interdependent on each other. We bless the lives of others or we detract from it. We are blessed by the life of others or we reject it.

God seems to bless people and continues to do so, so that their goodness, their blessings may be used to edify others. He doesn't want us to be selfish. My goodness, He surely is not selfish with those who love Him. Even the worst of us has a multitude of blessings. He blesses us quite often through others and He blesses others through us—our actions, our time, our services.

Man was to be happy and have all he needed. You've heard the expression, "there ain't no free lunch." Well, I beg to differ. There certainly is. This whole earth and everything in it is a free lunch. Man is to receive God's blessings. Let's be thankful for them.

For He satisfieth the longing soul,
and filleth the hungry soul with goodness.
Psalms 107:9

Godly Priorities

Once again, back to Adam we go. We must look at God's dealings with other men if we are to see how we fit, and see ways to deal with the blessings of this earth:

27 **So God created man in His own image, in the image of God created He him; male and female created He them.**

28 **And God blessed them, and God said unto them, Be fruitful, and multiply, and replenish the earth, and subdue it: and have dominion over the fish of the sea, and over the fowl of the air, and over every living thing that moveth upon the earth.**

Genesis 1:27-28

Leaping 4,000 years ahead, let's look at Paul's comments to the Corinthians. This is a great scripture:

8 **And God is able to make all grace abound toward you; that ye, always having all sufficiency in all things, may abound to every good work.**

9 **(As it is written, He hath dispersed abroad; He hath given to the poor; His righteousness remaineth for ever.**

10 Now He that ministereth seed to the sower both minister bread for your food, and multiply your seed sown, and increase the fruits of your righteousness;)

2 Corinthians 9:8-10

There's a semicolon here so we'll pick up the scripture in a moment. Let's look back at these verses. The word "abound" has an interesting meaning. My *American Heritage College Dictionary* defines it thusly: "To be great in number or amount; to be fully supplied or filled." How is it that God deals continually with man? In abundance. Jesus understood this well. How often did He feed His followers before He taught them? Sometimes the feeding itself became a great message.

Verses nine and ten deal once again with the material and the spiritual. It is abundantly clear (pardon the quick turnaround use of this word) that righteousness is the most important part of this.

The same message—love God, obey the commandments, love each other—are repeated throughout His works. But everything involves more: words like "multiply" and "increase" are used in the same sentence. Seeds become bread for food.

Verse 11 of 2 Corinthians 9 says, "Being enriched in every thing to all bountifulness, which causeth through us thanksgiving to God."

Several years ago, I received a Sunday School manual on "giving thanks," from a different church than mine. I was following Paul's advice to seek after every good thing. I loved the message of thanksgiving. I just happened to be back in my hometown of Tacoma, Washington. I was staying near Wapato Park, a lake (swamp) setting with a long foot bridge at one end. The message of this book, virtually every lesson, was about thanksgiving. The lessons were "Praising God," "Living With a Thankful Heart," "Counting Blessings," "Prayers of Thanksgiving," and so forth. The skies were swirling, all shapes of clouds were passing overhead. The sun shone brightly through—one of those scenes where the rays shine though. It had just rained and the air was pure. The trees, the lake—it was all beautiful. I stopped my jogging and stood all alone on the bridge. I raised my voice in a prayer—a prayer of awe, and a prayer of thanksgiving, a prayer of renewal and praise.

Daily, I added things to be thankful for. I counted my many blessings, one by one. I saw differently other people's kindnesses. I appreciated this country more. I was filled with a love for my wife and children. I was thankful for great things like the warmth of sunshine and the fact that my car started every morning. My attitude picked up my business. We've brought a lot of profits to the bottom line. Our company truly helps countless thousands of people. I was thankful for that. In fact, I have lived a life of abundance since that time. For me, it all started with a thankful heart.

That is not where it ended. Thank heaven for, line upon line, here a little and there a little . . .. Once you start down this path, many more ideas (scriptures) unfold. I'll tell more of my personal story elsewhere and only in places where changes, or turning points in my life might aid others. I am not finished. I am still on the road.

Riches of Old

Not all people in the Old Testament were rich. However, God's people always seemed to have sufficient wealth. Even in hard times like war and famine, He succored them. The whole story of Moses leading the people out of Egypt is priceless. Or of Joseph feeding his nation and his family throughout the seven years of famine.

Let's review a few Biblical references of wealth and prosperity. We'll use the word "rich" as our operative word for this discussion:

2   **And Abram was very rich in cattle, in silver, and in gold.**

Genesis 13:2

We have discussed Abraham before. I'll not add more here:

> 7   The Lord maketh poor, and maketh rich: He
>   bringeth low, and lifteth up.

1 Samuel 2:7

He has placed in motion so many awesome things. You have to pick up your Bible and read the next three verses. It's as if He does all this so we will call on Him. He wants us to rely on Heaven, and work for Him. We are not alone, He is with us, but He is strict:

> 30 Wherefore the Lord God of Israel saith, I said
>   indeed that thy house and the house of thy
>   father, should walk before me for ever: but
>   now the Lord saith, Be it far from me; for them
>   that honour me I will honour, and they that
>   despise me shall be lightly esteemed.

1 Samuel 2:30

> 4   He becometh poor that dealeth with a slack
>   hand: but the hand of the diligent maketh
>   rich.

Proverbs 10:4

It is up to us to be wise, to use our talents, to call upon and rely on the Lord and to walk uprightly. In and out of the church are people who deal with slack hands—usually sitting next to one who is diligent. You will recognize them by their fruits. This discourse is about prosperity and the good it comes from and the good it brings. Listen to this:

> 7   When a man's ways please the Lord, He
>   maketh even his enemies to be at peace with
>   him.

Proverbs 16:7

It would be interesting to use the past few verses and have a group discussion of the meaning, or importance of any of this. We act out what we think. We bridge ideas based on experiences and sometimes on how or what we want the results to be. Not all people want to prosper. Not all want the riches of eternity. Some people are so caught up in their ways they won't even contemplate a new or different life. God's ways are higher, but nowhere does it say we should not try to emulate them. Maybe we can't live "His ways" now, but does that mean we give up? We should have a diligent hand in learning and doing the will of God: "Be ye therefore perfect even as your Father which is in heaven is perfect," (Matthew 5:48) is not idle chatter: "Seeing then that all these things shall be dissolved, what manner of persons ought ye to be in all holy conversation and godliness." (II Peter 3:11)

I'm interested in this word "to be." It doesn't say set a goal "to be," or try "to be." But "to be." If you want to be thin, do what thin people do. If you want to be a basketball player, do what basketball players do. In the Hebrew language, there is no future tense conjugation of the verb "to be." It is all present. "To be" is to be right now. It is the essence of existence. If you want to be rich like Abraham or Jacob, then do what they did. Their lives are in the book. Look at the promise to them and to us. Look at the old covenant and the new covenant. Study their faith and their actions. You'll see a pattern.

God Makes a Covenant

God makes a covenant. It is important to Him. He does it repeatedly. The covenant is complete. Man's part is to walk in the covenant (words used to describe man's walk are uprightly, diligently, steadfast, et cetera). God blesses man with "exceeding wealth" and "every good thing." Man serves God by obeying the commandments. Part of this is to serve others (finding many good ways to do so).

Your story might be like Isaac's or like Joseph's. Your novel is being written. So is mine. I want the Lord to be the author of my story. I personally want to: "Commit thy works unto the Lord, and thy thoughts shall be established." (Proverbs 16:3) If we want to live God's way, we must have established thoughts—we do so by being committed to good works.

I am bewildered when I see people living with less than what they could have. When "lack or poverty" enters, it's amazing what we learn to tolerate. We need to change this way of thinking. When we get sick we do what we can to overcome it. We take pills, pray, ask for blessings, et cetera. We are often earnest in this endeavor. When we get sick spiritually, we should put forth similar effort. Likewise, when we get sick financially, we should surely try to get out of the sickness. Definitely, God wants to bless us in this department. He wants to bless us completely. His thoughts and actions to us are whole, they are complete, they are all inclusive.

We shouldn't feel that we are only entitled to part of God's blessings. We should seek every good gift. He will bless us immensely until our storehouse can't hold it all:

> 27 **Let them shout for joy, and be glad, that favour my righteous cause; yea, let them say continually, Let the Lord be magnified, which hath pleasure in the prosperity of His servant.**

> **Psalms 35:27**

It would serve us well to memorize this verse. Magnify God, be His servant and our prosperity will be pleasurable to Him.

His lord said unto him,
Well done, thou good and faithful servant:
thou hast been faithful over a few things,
I will make thee ruler over many things:
enter thou into the joy of thy lord.
Matthew 25:21

The Talents

The conclusion to this chapter is very important. It will provide a workable framework for the achievement of excellence. It is necessary to go through a set of scriptures, explore them as we go, and then make this conclusion.

There are two places where the story of the ten talents or pounds is told. One begins in Matthew 25:14, and the other is Luke 19:12. The account in Luke uses much more vivid language, and also changes the basis and return on investment, as in Matthew. The story in Matthew is the more common account. I'll list them here side by side.

There are some obvious differences. "Why?" You may ask. Well, they are told by two different people, probably at completely different times. One was probably heard directly from the mouth of Jesus, the other related by a third party.

However, even though there are differences in the verses, and how the story goes, there are no differences in the outcome—what the master said and what he did. It's pretty incredible to see these accounts side by side. There is a treasure chest of knowledge here.

I won't belabor here the value of a talent, only to say it was a measurement of money. A talent today is usually the ability to do something in a special way. If the reader wants to marry these two concepts together it is fine, as it may give depth to our desire to develop our abilities.

Matthew:

14 For the kingdom of heaven is as a man travelling into a far country, who called his own servants, and delivered unto them his goods.

15 And unto one he gave five talents, to another two, and to another one; to every man according to his several ability; and straightway took his journey.

16 Then he that had received the five talents went and traded with the same, and made them other five talents.

17 And likewise he that had received two, he also gained other two.

18 But he that had received one went and digged in the earth, and hid his Lord's money.

19 After a long time the Lord of those servants cometh, and reckoneth with them.

20 And so he that had received five talents came and brought other five talents, saying, Lord, thou deliveredst unto me five talents: behold, I have gained beside them five talents more.

21 His Lord said unto him, Well done, thou good and faithful servant: thou hast been faithful over a few

Luke:

12 He said therefore, A certain noble man went into a far country to receive for himself a kingdom, and to return.

13 And he called his ten servants, and delivered them ten pounds, and said unto them, Occupy till I come.

15 And it came to pass, that when he was returned, having received the kingdom, then he commanded these servants to be called unto him, to whom he had given the money, that he might know how much every man had gained by trading.

things, I will make thee ruler over many things: enter thou into the joy of thy Lord.

22 He also that had received two talents came and said, Lord, thou deliveredst unto me two talents: behold, I have gained two other talents beside them.

23 His Lord said unto him, Well done, good and faithful servant; thou hast been faithful over a few things, I will make thee ruler over many things: enter thou into the joy of thy Lord.

24 Then he which had received the one talent came and said, Lord, I knew thee that thou art an hard man, reaping where thou hast not sown, and gathering where thou hast not strawed:

25 And I was afraid, and went and hid thy talent in the earth: lo, there thou hast that is thine.

26 His Lord answered and said unto him, Thou wicked and slothful servant, thou knewest that I reap where I sowed not, and gather where I have not strawed:

27 Thou oughtest therefore to have put my money

16 Then came the first, saying, Lord, thy pound hath gained ten pounds.

17 And he said unto him, Well, thou good servant: because thou hast been faithful in a very little, have thou authority over ten cities.

18 And the second came, saying, Lord, thy pound hath gained five pounds.

19 And he said likewise to him, Be thou also over five cities.

20 And another came, saying, Lord, behold, here is thy pound, which I have kept laid up in a napkin:

21 For I feared thee, because thou art an austere man: thou takest up that thou layedst not down, and reapest that thou didst not sow.

22 And he saith unto him, Out of thine own mouth will I judge thee, thou wicked servant. Thou knewest that I was an austere man, taking up that I laid not down, and reaping that I did not sow:

23 Wherefore then gavest not thou my money into the bank, that at my

to the exchangers, and then at my coming I should have received mine own with usury.

28 Take therefore the talent from him, and give it unto him which hath ten talents.

29 For unto every one that hath shall be given, and he shall have abundance: but from him that hath not shall be taken away even that which he hath.

Matthew 25:14-29

coming I might have required mine own with usury?

24 And he said unto them that stood by, Take from him the pound, and give it to him that hath ten pounds.
25 (And they said unto him, Lord, he hath ten pounds.)
26 For I say unto you, That unto every one which hath shall be given; and from him that hath not, even that he hath shall be taken away from him.

Luke 19:12-26

Commentary

Both accounts have a master—a land owner or employer—leaving. In Matthew (vs. 14), he gives his goods to his servants. In Luke he gives ten pounds to ten different servants. He gives one pound to each, or we are to suppose this, because as he asks for them to account for their pound, he calls three, and each tells what he did with his pound. In Matthew, one servant is given five talents, one two talents, and the third receives one talent.

Almost all masters, or bosses, want to know how their employees will perform. When I leave town, I give assignments and often set the stage—usually by giving a responsibility to someone to see how they do. Upon my return, I don't always have to ask for an accounting, the results are usually visible. The assignment is clear. These servants are to improve their lot. To use a way overused word, they are *empowered*.

Also, note in Matthew (vs. 15) the expression "according to his several ability." How I wish our do-gooders in government office would realize this and not expect people to be the same (equal) and then manipulate people through programs to output or have equal results. Life is not like that, neither are the true message of the scriptures.

Let's explore the results of Matthew first. The one with five "traded with the same and made them another five talents." The one with two "gained" two more. The one with one "digged in the earth and hid his Lord's money." He buried it. How sad. I meet people all the time who hide their talents. They bury a part of themselves. They do not know how great it can be—how great they can be. To take any physical talent, spiritual gift, or monetary resource and do nothing is truly a shame. No wonder the master used the word "slothful." A time of reckoning will come. Verse 19 says, "the Lord of those servants cometh, and reckoneth with them."

Now, let's see what the Lord says and moreover, what he does. This has to make people in government cringe. It is so against what bleeding heart do-gooders say and do.

The one with five came and brought the other five—his return on investments, or the profit of his labor. "I have gained beside them five talents more." Listen to the response of his Lord, "Well done, thou good and faithful servant: thou hast been faithful over a few things, I will make thee ruler over many things: enter thou into the joy of the Lord."

Is there any more wonderful sentence that could be said to any of us who strive to be obedient, to serve the Lord? Tell me words that you want to hear more than to "enter into the joy of the Lord." To have a place with him, on his terms, having humbly obeyed, having done well in developing our talents and gifts—and having returned all, the original sum, plus the gain, back to him to use as he sees fit. The same is said to the servant who gives two talents. He gained and returned two more. But now the plot thickens. What of those who do nothing? Who, for whatever reason, fail to develop their talents?

24 Lord, I knew thee that thou art an hard man, reaping where thou hast not sown, and gathering where thou hast not strawed.

25 And I was afraid and went and hid thy talent in the earth: Lo, there thou hast that is thine.

Matthew 25:24-25

This is not what the Lord wanted. It probably is not what this servant wanted, especially if he was able to view the other two making profits or "reckonings." Fear stopped him. He was more afraid of what the Lord would do if he lost it than not returning a gain.

Here an interesting point: there is no mention of a servant who tried to get gain but lost. I wonder how the Lord would respond? I can't imagine a master punishing a servant if the person honestly tried; with wisdom, with diligence and love. In both accounts, the first two seemed to have used a sure (tried and true) method. I can't speculate His response only to extrapolate from other scriptures his responses of losing all to gain all, and his comments of forgiveness.

26 **Thou wicked and slothful servant, thou knewest that I reap where I sowed not, and gather where I have not strawed:**

27 **Thou oughtest therefore to have put my money to the exchangers, and then at my coming I should have received mine own with usury.**

Matthew 25:26-27

"Usury" here being interest paid, or a return for the use of the money. I can't imagine usury being a doubling of the money. He would have been happy with even a little.

Up until now, we have read what the Lord says. What uniquely vivid words they have been, but read now what he did—or commanded to be done. No imagery is needed. The action speaks volumes, "Take therefore the talent from him, and give it unto him which hath ten talents." Wow, and he goes on, "For unto every one that hath shall be given, and he shall have abundance: but from him that hath not shall be taken away even that which he hath." These words are so full of meaning. Again, we see the word abundance. Not scarcity, not just enough, but abundance. More than is necessary, more than enough. And to the fearful, the idle, they shall remain with nothing. Again, whether it's money, spiritual gifts, or abilities, if we don't use them, we lose them. There is a natural law here also. These things atrophy—they wither away.

I have tried to not make this a political book. My desire to not have government meddle in our lives is abundantly clear. Actually, I think activist government action causes so much damage. It hurts so deeply, and so lastingly, the people it purports to help. Couldn't it learn a lesson from the scriptures?

The master left those servants to their own ways—their own devices. They did not need forced training programs, a welfare safety net, minimum wage, or the promise of a never-ending income at age 65. They needed freedom to trade, freedom to be, and freedom from intrusion. So enough of my political incorrectness after this last statement.

Many poor will do nothing to get ahead. The people with wealth will build factories, create jobs and build up all who want to participate. Yes, there will always be poor—as some will hide their talents in the earth. The lord gave these three servants the opportunity to help build a bigger economic pie.

So, to those who think government knows best, re-read these scriptures and memorize them, but most importantly apply them. Good intentions, but wrong-headed processes spell disaster for so many.

I'm not done with this parable, there are a few things we still must learn from the account of Luke. I'll probably never be done trying to educate the elitist few who wreak havoc on us all because they do not know what the scriptures teach. Or worse, they have read the Bible but never stop to study what it says and apply it's principles to their lives.

Luke

In Luke, the servants' returns are substantially different. The first to make an accounting said, "Thy pound hath gained ten pounds." The second said, "Thy pound hath gained five pounds." We're talking a ten times increase, or 1000%, and a five times increase, or 500%. And we don't know how long this took, it could have been months—or even years.

I bring this up here and highlight those numbers for a personal reason. The five years before I wrote this book, I was, and still am, engaged in writing books, teaching seminars and workshops, and marketing a computer bulletin board service about the stock market.

I get fantastic returns on many of my trades. I show people how to take $10,000 and turn it into $30,000 in two to five months. My students excel, many quitting their jobs within weeks. When you apply the law of abundance, learn the secrets of the "exchangers" or "banks," you can profit immensely.

I have been so criticized by the powers that be. You cannot imagine how badly. I keep on churning out huge 10,280%, 3,874%, 140,680%, 2,845% annualized returns. Yes, I have a few losers, but overall, my results are spectacular (you can find my time-tested strategies in ***Real Estate Money Machine*** and ***Real Estate For Real People***, or in ***Wall Street Money Machine***, ***Stock Market Miracles***, and ***Bear Market Baloney***).

I commend my detractors to Luke 19:16—a 1,000% return. And I commend all of you to this thought process. If one becomes ten, then ten becomes one hundred—and it's going to keep going. Just think of the tithing you can pay.

In Luke, the slothful servant hides the money in a napkin. For Pete's sake—a napkin! The servant was afraid; this time, he said the master was an "austere" man.

The Lord says the same thing, but this time calls him a "wicked" servant. Then, watch what happens as he commands others to take the one pound and give it to the one with ten (again, take note welfare statists and wealth redistributionists everywhere). In Luke 19, verse 25, the scriptures confirm this. Read verses 25 and 26 again, and notice the master's response:

25 (And they said unto him, Lord, he hath ten pounds.)

26 For I say unto you, That unto every one which hath shall be given; and from him that hath not, even what he hath shall be taken away from him.

Luke 19:25-26

What a bunch of cry babies. They can't believe the Lord really meant to take the one pound away (so he's left with nothing) and give to the new rich guy. Wow, does the Lord have his own "redistribution of wealth" system? No wonder so many of these people in government want nothing to do with the Bible.

Something is expected of all of us. If we need to find the road to heaven, we must begin now. If we should be bettering our family, then to hide our talents is "wicked," and we should start using our talents immediately. If it's to prosper and live a life of abundance, then we must begin.

I love my chosen occupation, because my company can and does help so many start on the road to wealth enhancement. If you have much (like the one with five talents) then more is expected. Look at the middle part of Luke 12:

48 But he that knew not, and did commit things worthy of stripes, shall be beaten with few stripes. For unto whomsoever much is given, of him shall much be required: and to whom men have committed much, of him they will ask the more.

Luke 12:48

I can't add any insights that will help. Read and memorize this scripture. And most importantly strive to be the one who does more. Then you will be asked to do more—you'll find yourself in a wonderful cycle of accomplishments.

And my final word on this subject, which I hope brings us all back to the spiritual aspect of this is 1 Timothy 4:14, which says: "Neglect not the gift that is in thee . . . ."

9

I have shewed you all things,
how that so labouring ye ought to
support the weak, and to remember
the words of the Lord Jesus, how He said,
It is more blessed to give than to receive.
Acts 20:35

The Gift Of Giving

All throughout the Bible, and to a lesser extent in this book, there is the call to walk in God's ways, to follow Him.

It seems that a broad view of this would be to take as important that which God takes as important—take seriously that which He takes seriously. There are hundreds of "to do" things and hundreds of "thou shalts" and "thou shalt nots." I think we can, however, categorize all of these into three areas: 1) Love God. Devote yourself to Him. Think on Him. Worship Him. 2) Obey the commandments. Learn, love, and live His laws. 3) Be careful in our relationships to others, including family. Love others as ourselves. Be one with one another:

> 12 **This is my commandment, That ye love one another, as I have loved you.**
>
> **John 15:12**

The following remarks are given to expand on loving one another. Our foundation has to be God's way and His methods for dealing with us. As we've closely studied, He blesses us through the covenant of Abraham. If we do our part, He delights in blessing and prospering us.

He is willing to, and in fact does, give us everything. There is in His Kingdom a plan of salvation and wealth sufficient for all of us.

Right now, I'm sitting in a Carl Jr.'s in southern California. I'm at the corner of Western and Sunset Boulevard. It's early. I'm here in Los Angeles to be interviewed on a TV show. There is this chapter on giving and two or three more chapters to write before this book is ready to go to press. I was going to say finished, but I don't know if I'll ever be finished.

The drive from Orange County was beautiful. The sun was rising in the east. The trees were blossoming. Yes, there are more beautiful places on this earth than the asphalt jungle of southern California, but I felt good. Thanksgiving filled my heart. I was grateful for a mind that lets me think about and remember other places. I looked all around. We truly are blessed.

I'm sitting here surrounded by several ethnic groups. I hear several different languages being spoken. I love the study of foreign languages. I especially love English, my own tongue, but it's great to hear all of these people. I love this melting pot. I hope one day to hear God's pure language. What a thrill that will be for me.

Maybe it's selfish, but I often think of how God blesses us—how He blesses me. I wonder how I can be a blessing to Him. I'm into asset building. I spend my working time building assets and showing people how to build, then protect their assets. I believe God will protect us as we do all we can. We need to build a city with a strong wall.

Assets? I wonder what kind of an asset I am to Him who has everything. He has given us the law of tithing. Repeatedly throughout the Bible there are references to giving. Does He really need my one-tenth? Will He get by without it? The answer is no, He does not need my tithe, and yes, He can do without it easily. Then why have the law? My conjecture is that the law is for us directly and for others indirectly. He gives us His all. He wants so little in return—financially that is. What He wants is our hearts—our devotion. With each increase, He wants us to think of Him. He is a jealous God, but He is a loving God. Our offerings are used to further His work. If we do our part, then countless other people in innumerable ways are helped.

Reread where God says, " ... prove me now herewith." What a statement! What a challenge! He says that, if we do what He asks, we can watch and see Him prove His word true. He is always true. This is a wonderful part of the covenant.

The poor will always be with us. Remember the stories in the New Testament which dealt with Jesus and what people did for Him? A woman anointed His feet with an expensive ointment and bathed His feet with her hair. He was challenged by one of His apostles. Shouldn't we take this oil, sell it and give to the poor? Jesus' answer is astonishing. Let's read the account:

3 **Then took Mary a pound of ointment of spikenard, very costly, and anointed the feet of Jesus, and wiped his feet with her hair: and the house was filled with the odour of the ointment.**

4 **Then saith one of His disciples, Judas Iscariot, Simon's son, which should betray him,**

5 **Why was not this ointment sold for three hundred pence, and given to the poor?**

6 **This he said, not that he cared for the poor; but because he was a thief, and had the bag, and bare what was put therein.**

7 **Then said Jesus, Let her alone: against the day of my burying hath she kept this.**

8 **For the poor always ye have with you; but me ye have not always.**

John 12:3-8

It was Judas Iscariot who asked about the poor. We don't need to wonder where his heart was. Did he really want to give to the poor? Look at verse six: He "had his bag." He controlled the money. Shortly he would disgracefully betray the Master for thirty pieces of silver. (It was that Mary which anointed the Lord with ointment, and wiped His feet with her hair, whose brother Lazarus was sick). (John 11:2)

There are so many lessons to learn here. Mary's heart was right. I'm sure it had to be. This small "donation" would not affect the poor one way or the other, but she needed it. We need to do likewise.

There is another account in Luke of a woman anointing Jesus with ointment. It is most beautiful and once again, the spirit will touch us with personal inspiration to behave differently when we see this action and reaction. Read these words slowly and carefully:

36 **And one of the Pharisees desired Him that He would eat with him. And He went into the Pharisee's house, and sat down to meat.**

37 **And, behold, a woman in the city, which was a sinner, when she knew that Jesus sat at meat in the Pharisee's house, brought an alabaster box of ointment,**

38 **And stood at His feet behind him weeping, and began to wash His feet with tears, and did wipe them with the hairs of her head, and kissed His feet, and anointed them with the ointment.**

39 **Now when the Pharisee which had bidden Him saw it, he spake within himself, saying, This Man, if He were a prophet, would have known who and what manner of woman this is that toucheth Him: for she is a sinner.**

40 **And Jesus answering said unto him, Simon, I have somewhat to say unto thee. And he saith, Master, say on.**

41 There was a certain creditor which had two debtors: the one owed five hundred pence, and the other fifty.

42 And when they had nothing to pay, he frankly forgave them both. Tell me therefore, which of them will love him most?

43 Simon answered and said, I suppose that he, to whom he forgave most. And he said unto him, Thou hast rightly judged.

44 And he turned to the woman, and said unto Simon, Seest thou this woman? I entered into thine house, thou gavest me no water for my feet: but she hath washed my feet with tears, and wiped them with the hairs of her head.

45 Thou gavest me no kiss: but this woman since the time I came in hath not ceased to kiss my feet.

46 My head with oil thou didst not anoint: but this woman hath anointed my feet with ointment.

47 Wherefore I say unto thee, Her sins, which are many, are forgiven; for she loved much: but to whom little is forgiven, the same loveth little.

48 And he said unto her, Thy sins are forgiven.

49 And they that sat at meat with him began to say within themselves, Who is this that forgiveth sins also?

50 And he said to the woman, Thy faith hath saved thee; go in peace.

Luke 7:36-50

This woman was a sinner. Aren't we all? The Pharisee questioned Him, how self-righteous! Jesus wanted to set Simon, the Pharisee, straight. He questions Simon: "There was a certain creditor which had two debtors: the one owed five hundred pence, and the other fifty. And when they had nothing to pay, he frankly forgave them both. Tell me therefore, which of them will love him most?" (Luke 7:41, 42) Simon answered correctly—the one he forgave the most.

The gift of forgiveness is a wonderful gift. It brings peace. "And He said to the woman, Thy faith hath saved thee; go in peace." (Luke 7:50) I know, in my own life, that when I ask forgiveness, I appreciate this healing power ever the more if the sin I committed was more serious.

I sincerely hope this story touches you as it does me. I wonder if my heart is in the right place. Do I feel such great remorse as this woman did? Am I willing to give my best to the Lord? What kind of "peculiar treasure" can I be for Him or give to Him today?

Back to Basics

There will be ample opportunities to be a help in the lives of others. We should look for opportunities. But we should also do the basics: Pay an honest tithe. Pay it completely. Pay it in a timely manner. And pay it joyfully.

God says:

> 7 **Even from the days of your fathers ye are gone away from mine ordinances, and have not kept them. Return unto me, and I will return unto you, saith the Lord of hosts. But ye said, Wherein shall we return?**
>
> **Malachi 3:7**

And then a very often quoted scripture:

> 8 **Will a man rob God? Yet ye have robbed me.**

God didn't want any confusion on this matter, so He asked another question and gave a definitive answer:

> 8 **But ye say, Wherein have we robbed thee? In tithes and offerings.**
>
> **Malachi 3:8**

He then proceeds to tell us exactly what to do. He gives a commandment followed by a wonderful reward. A blessing and reward worthy of Abraham.

"Bring ye all the tithes into the storehouse," (note, He did not say part, and He did not say that we can distribute our money—tithes—as we see fit. We are to give them to His storehouse, "that there may be meat in mine house, and prove me now herewith, saith the Lord of hosts, if I will not open you the windows of heaven, and pour you out a blessing, that there shall not be room enough to receive it." (Malachi 3:10) What could this mean? Pour out blessing from Heaven could mean a better job, a bumper crop, a successful business or career—whatever it will be, it will be from Him and done His way. He now tells how large this blessing will be. Remember, He asks a tithe—or one-tenth, and offerings. Here's how big, "that there shall not be room enough to receive it."

Wow? And double wow! I can hardly hold back my enthusiasm for this scripture. It's simply wonderful. I know it has been true in my life. I wrote about this in the chapter, "Multiplication." I sit here today not able to hold it all. This is a blessing available to all of us. It is powerful. It is complete and it definitely is achievable. Think of God first. Don't get paid first, or run your business and pay God if there is anything left over. Pay Him first.

Recently I was teaching some of these principles in a stock market/asset protection/tax class, and I mentioned the Girl Scouts. A man told me something during the break. I'll tell you what he said, but let me first tell you my remarks during the class so you can see what lead up to his comments:

Several years ago, a girl scout outside Safeway wanted me to buy some cookies. I bought seven boxes for $21. She just stared at me. Most people walk on by. If they do stop, they buy one box. I went to my car. I looked back and she ran to her mother and from a distance I could see her telling her about me. She didn't know me, but I'm sure the $21 had a dramatic impact in her life.

Now, every time I pass a bake sale, or car wash, or Boy Scout raffle tickets, I buy, or just give them $20. Sometimes more. It certainly does have an impact on them. Try it. You will always have another $20 to give. Maybe a hundredfold. You will make an impact in their lives.

In the hallway, this stately gentleman—by his looks, very successful—said, "Wade, I can't prove this by the scriptures, but it seems God has a reverse law of tithing." My interest was piqued. We talked for quite a while. His thoughts were, "If you'll give a little, God blesses with a lot. If you have increase, He expects a tithing. If you pay your full share, He blesses you with ten times more." I thought and thought on this. You know, it doesn't sound too different than the one hundredfold return.

Let's run the numbers (this is the most famous expression from our Wall Street Workshop). If you make $10,000 and pay $1,000 in tithing and then if you are blessed with 10 times more, that's $100,000. That's 100 times the $1,000 you paid in.

You can't find those exact numbers in the Bible, but you will find a God ready to give us His all. A God who gives increase, a God who multiplies. A God who wants the covenant of Abraham to be alive in our lives.

As a business person, our first expenditure should be a cheerful gift back to Him who provides everything. We need to do this to keep our heart in the right place. He will bless us and others according to His good pleasure.

You would have to look a long time in the Bible to find words where people are told to brag or to show off their actions, especially in giving to the poor or in making offerings. Once in awhile, Jesus told people to go and tell someone of the good thing that was done to them, but when it comes to giving alms or prayer openly, people are told to do so in their closet. In private.

I don't see the Lord condemning group or public prayer or discussions as He prayed and did many things in the open quite frequently, but I do see Him telling people not to brag, or gloat. This story proves the point:

1 Take heed that ye do not your alms before men, to be seen of them: otherwise ye have no reward of your Father which is in heaven.

2 Therefore when thou doest thine alms, do not sound a trumpet before thee, as the hypocrites do in the synagogues and in the streets, that they may have glory of men. Verily I say unto you, They have their reward.

3 But when thou doest alms, let not thy left hand know what thy right hand doeth:

4 That thine alms may be in secret: and thy Father which seeth in secret himself shall reward thee openly.

Matthew 6:1-4

Where is your reward? Where do you want it to be? It is not always easy to walk uprightly. It is not easy to withhold judgment. For example, it is easy to love those who love us. It is easy to be friendly to those who are friendly to us. It is easy to be around people who dress like us and have the same attitudes. Many people do this. Look at Deuteronomy, Chapter 10:17-19:

17 For the Lord your God is God of gods, and Lord of lords, a great God, a mighty, and a terrible, which regardeth not persons, nor taketh reward:

18 He doth execute the judgment of the fatherless and widow, and loveth the stranger, in giving him food and raiment.

19 Love ye therefore the stranger: for ye were strangers in the land of Egypt.

Deuteronomy 10:17-19

Higher ways, indeed. In another place, the Lord asks: "How is the faithful city become an harlot! it was full of judgment; righteousness lodged in it; but now murderers." (Isaiah 1:21) The answer said this, "Thy princes are rebellious, and companions of thieves: every one loveth gifts, and followeth after rewards: they judge not the fatherless, neither doth the cause of the widow come unto them." (Isaiah 1:23) These rewards and gifts are about ill-gotten gains. There is no place for these in the hearts of people trying to do His will. We definitely are not to take advantage of others. Proverbs 22:22 says: "Rob not the poor, because he is poor: neither oppress the afflicted in the gate." It's interesting to note in the next verse how similar the words are to those which we just read in Deuteronomy. Words that say the Lord will take up the poor's cause because they can't. Verse 23 of Proverbs 22 says: "For the Lord will plead their cause, and spoil the soul of those that spoiled them." More food for thought is Proverbs 14:20: "The poor is hated even of his own neighbour: but the rich hath many friends." The question is not why but what are we going to do about it?

The type of reward we seek should be like Psalms 31:23, which states: "O love the Lord, all ye His saints: for the Lord preserveth the faithful, and plentifully rewardeth the proud doer." Remember though, not to sound a trumpet.

Look at the man Cornelius in Acts 10:2: "A devout man, and one that feared God with all his house, which gave much alms to the people, and prayed to God alway." He put to work his devotion. His giving was important to him, as he gave "much." And to think he was a centurion in the Roman Empire. His unit was called "the Italian band."

The Lord accepts good will from all sources. Cornelius went to Peter. He knew that Jews should not hang out with men like him. He told Peter of an experience he had, "And Cornelius said, Four days ago I was fasting until this hour; and at the ninth hour I prayed in my house, and behold, a man stood before me in bright clothing, And said, Cornelius, thy prayer is heard, and thine alms are had in remembrance in the sight of God." (Acts 10:30-31)

Does God have us in His sights? Peter's answer is really great: "Then Peter opened his mouth, and said, Of a truth I perceive that God is no respecter of persons: But in every nation he that feareth Him, and worketh righteousness, is accepted with Him." (Acts 10:34-35)

Remember 1 Samuel 2:30: "Wherefore the Lord God of Israel saith, I said indeed that thy house, and the house of thy father, should walk before me for ever: but now the Lord saith, Be it far from me; for them that honour me I will honour." He asks so little financially, but He rewards us His way—which is exceedingly great.

Because the government has access to our books—especially when we die—many strange and great things are uncovered. From time to time I read of a deceased person who has spent a life giving and helping others. A life, directly and indirectly, of donating time and money to various people and causes. And not done so for corporate advertising or gain. They humbly and quietly went about their business. In fact, they did so anonymously very often. Not even the charity (or whoever) knew who the donor was. It would be hard to keep it a secret anyway, once people knew. But they did not want recognition. Recognition was not their reason for giving.

Let me give an example. The founder of Wrigley gum built a great company. He helped others, gave to charities, and was "proud" to pay his taxes. He felt it was un-American to use asset protection devices. Do you wonder what the government did for him when he died? Remember, this is after years of service, bond drives, chairing major causes, and making patriotic contributions. The government decimated his estate. They left his family and his business nearly bankrupt. I'll talk more about this is the taxation chapter.

I don't think there is anything wrong with small open gifts or large gifts like a wing on a hospital—and having one's name put on it. However, we should search our hearts and determine our motivation, then follow the course that puts rewards in proper perspective:

> 23 Thus saith the Lord, Let not the wise man glory in his wisdom, neither let the mighty man glory in his might, let not the rich man glory in his riches:

24 But let him that glorieth glory in this, that he understandeth and knoweth me, that I am the Lord which exercise loving kindness, judgment, and righteousness, in the earth: for in these things I delight, saith the Lord.

Jeremiah 9:23-24

What a wonderful recipe for happiness! Let's make sure we delight in the same things the Lord does.

10

*The rich ruleth over the poor,
and the borrower is
servant to the lender.
Proverbs 22:7*

A Word About Debt

There are not a lot of references to debt in the Bible. The few that exist make it clear, when put in context, that God's concern is that we not put ourselves in bondage. To do so might cause us to do strange things.

I think today, God would be just as concerned with drugs. They bind people down. They are like anything else that causes us to turn from God. God's music is one beautiful and consistent refrain. Satan's music is varied and raucous. There are many arrows in Satan's quiver (sin, despondency, pride, anger, coveting, et cetera) and it matters not which one he uses if he can get us to go off the mark—or shoot beyond it, or fall short of it.

Debt is just such a thing if it is not handled properly. Debt can become a bondage. It can get us to do things we normally wouldn't do. Debt can get us off course. In the Old Testament there are references to lending. There are scriptures which say to lend and others which say not to. Paul admonishes us to "Owe no man any thing, but to love one another: for he that loveth another hath fulfilled the law." (Romans 13:8) This would be an easy scripture to take out of context and to do so, I think, would be a mistake. Don't get me wrong, I loath debt, and furthermore, I think it is a killer of businesses. I will say more on this later.

7 Render therefore to all their dues: tribute to whom tribute is due; custom to whom custom; fear to whom fear; honour to whom honour.

8 Owe no man any thing, but to love one another: for he that loveth another hath fulfilled the law.

Romans 13:7-8

Paul is writing to the Romans, and in this part of chapter 13, he is dealing with being subject to leaders. He admonishes them to pay tribute to God's ministers and, in verse seven, lists several things they are to do. Then he finishes verse eight with his continued exhortation to love one another. It's as if being in debt would hurt this attempt.

Jesus never told anyone to not be in debt. In fact, He used debt and money examples frequently. His concern, and I think Paul's, too, is that we focus on that which is right. We need to set our heart on God, and anything, including debt, which detracts from that is bad.

Mature Debt Society

Today, our debt factories are pervasive. We live in a mature debt economy. Just because debt is all around us, we do not have to participate. I think it's cute when I hear or read of people cutting up their credit cards. If that's what they have to do to get control, then so be it. It's about control and staying focused. It's not about cutting up credit cards.

I was as guilty as anyone. When young, and upon receiving my first major department store credit card, I ran it up. I mean I was at my limit in days. Not only did the bill come at the wrong time, but the interest rate was high. I stopped using it. I paid off the bill over several months, then only used it sparingly.

There is an agreement between the lender and the lendee. If you are comfortable, and it's not excessive—if you are using a credit card for convenience—then it just becomes another medium of exchange. It is when you abuse the privilege and overextend past your ability to repay that you truly are in bondage—or debt.

I know that debt is a touchy subject. I've talked to dozens of people about it and the responses were varied and most interesting. All agree debt can be bad. Most feel that to live a life free of any type of bondage is good. Debt, if you're in control, does not represent bondage. Let me use buying a home as an example. I believe in possessing land. So does God. Land and ownership is big to Him. He prepared land for His people and He prepared ways for them to get it.

There are two types of debt which I feel, if controlled, are okay. One is a mortgage to buy your own home. The other is investment or business debt.

I also believe in the law of abundance, of hundredfold returns. You can pay off the mortgage early. Be dedicated to the cause. See Appendix B for a plan to do so. Simply put, you can gang up on the principal payment.

I don't think of this as debt so long as the property covers the mortgage—the property owes it, if you will. I know this is a stretch, but it allows people to render to Caesar less money—interest is tax deductible. It adds stability and causes us not to have to rent, or be moved, when we don't want to. If I owe $150,000 on a home and the house is worth $200,000 then fine. If I can comfortably make the $1,400 payments, then this is not bondage.

Business Debt

The second possibility for debt is business debt. I think strategic business debt might be necessary, but it is where I see a lot of misery. It is one of the components I use in my stock market seminars in evaluating companies. Does their debt load make it hard to function and grow? Debt is a killer of businesses. Even if a company is making money, excessive debt can drive it into insolvency and possibly into bankruptcy.

Please allow me to refer to my own story once again. In 1993, my wife and I and our children moved back to Washington state. I love it here. We had been living in Arizona. I was speaking for a company headquartered here and was doing quite well—making $300,000 to $400,000 a year. I had a desire to go back into business, knowing I could grow a company, create jobs, and help more people than we were currently helping.

My wife and I talked about it extensively. One promise I made to her upon leaving Arizona (actually it was a bribe to encourage her to want to move) was that she would not have to work the business. For years, she had helped out. Often she was stuck with all the junk stuff—the taxes, the bills, and the like. I got all the glory—speaking to great audiences, writing the books.

Now, she felt a need to be at home totally with the kids. It was a wonderful decision by a wonderful person. Now, we have our last three in home school. It is full-time for her to be with them, take care of our horse farm, get the kids in horse shows, and all of her other church responsibilities. It is a most interesting life and we are both happier.

The business blossomed, by the way. It's not that she's home taking care of her "business," but that I also found the right people to help the business flourish. Again, God gives us what we need.

There were two more promises I made her: 1) We wouldn't go into any business debt. If we needed a computer or a phone system we would pay cash. No financing. 2) I would keep the business under five employees.

Well, in a month I had to go and ask if that second point could be extended. We both looked at the income, the needs, the potential and she trusted me to do what was right.

The first year, we did $780,000 in sales, the second year $2,800,000. The third year was $7,400,000 and the next year was $46,500,000. The projection for this year is about double that. We have about 400 employees and outside contractors.

It has been done with no debt. Our bills are paid. Recently we bought a 61,000 square foot office building. We used some mortgage debt after putting almost a million dollars into it. We remodeled with $2,500,000, and did it from cash flow—no debt. We have purchased all of, or parts of six major hotels and have put over $4,000,000 into investments. We continue to grow—all without the bondage of debt. We are ganging up on the mortgage, paying down on our building and on the hotels.

Most of my business associates think that carrying more debt is okay. I say no. Profit Financial Corporation is the parent company. It is publicly traded. I guess we could expand faster if we used debt. I'm the Chairman of the Board, and I say, "No." We're expanding rapidly enough and we're doing so with profits, not loans. I only brought this up to show those of you who need this information that there is another way.

You see, if we have a slow month (which are few and far between) it matters not. We don't have a huge nut to crack. Shortly, we'll have the building paid off. We have no lease payments for equipment or bank loans. Neither I, nor anyone else, is a slave to this business. As a matter of fact, we are very successful. My passion for living a debt-free business life has had wonderful consequences. I only want to be in debt to God:

> **Oh, to grace how great a debtor**
> **Daily I'm constrained to be!**
> **Let thy goodness like a fetter,**
> **Bind my wandering heart to thee.**
> **"Come, Thou Fount"**
> **Robert Robinson**

This debt-free thinking has other ramifications. I wanted a business that would seriously help others. With each business endeavor, I've asked myself certain questions:

- Is it honest? Are all parts of it good and wholesome?
- Will it help others learn and grow and be better?

- Will it encourage family togetherness—kids working beside parents and grandparents?
- Will it help people pay more tithes and offerings?
- Will it encourage people to keep a holier Sabbath?
- Will it help people do well so they can do more good—service to others?
- Will it comply with, and abide by, the laws of God and draw people closer to Him?

My business does these. Every day I try to use the scriptures and principles of righteousness to further this cause. It started with a promise to let my wife stay at home and stay out of debt. It has grown from there.

Then He saith unto them,
Render therefore unto Caesar
the things which are Caesar's;
and unto God the things that are God's.
Matthew 22:21

Paying Caesar

This chapter will not be long, but the information is important. We live in this country and must abide by the laws. It is, however, our duty to understand the laws. It is almost impossible to understand the complex tax code. We must do our best. I try to help small business owners and small investors learn how to do this. I teach tax reduction, retirement planning, and asset protection seminars nationwide, even around the world.

My belief is that we are to enjoy the fruits of our labors. No one (except God) has the right to take these away from us and God wants us to give it cheerfully back to Him. He does not force us. He does not have revenue agents which can garnish wages, or put liens on our property, or extract money from our accounts, or padlock our doors. Government (especially in the United States with our great constitution) is to protect our individual rights. We have politicians elected to do just that and then move to Washington DC and take away our rights—specifically the right to use, spend, enjoy, and dispose of our assets and our investments. We should learn and use every possible part of the tax code which allows us to keep more of what we make.

In ancient times, the government was allowed to take one-tenth. Now remember, these writings (in other places besides the Bible) about government taxes (tribute) were about governments run by men of God. Once in awhile the government could take an additional one-fifth. This is usually in times of war or in times of feast preceding times of famine.

Also, the people of God were taxed one-tenth, the strangers in the land were taxed the one-tenth plus an additional one tenth or one fifth. This would be interesting. You see, America is a tax haven for thousands of foreigners. They come here, make money, and move it offshore. Let's tax legitimate, real Americans one rate and foreign companies another, or higher, rate. Let's copy the days of old.

There is one scripture of particular note in Proverbs. I came across this scripture by reading the Wall Street Journal. A Jewish Rabbi used it. His translation went something like this, "The hands of the diligent shall produce wealth, while the lazy shall pay taxes." The King James version says the same thing, but the language is a little hard to read:

24 **The hand of the diligent shall bear rule: but the slothful shall be under tribute.**

Proverbs 12:24

Would all activist government sympathizers, those who think that the government can take care of people better than people can care for themselves, please read this? Remember, when someone gets something they did not earn, then someone else earns something they don't get.

Wealthy people build factories, start businesses, invest and build the economy. The poor people I know want a better life, but they don't need handouts. They don't need the government confiscating property (money) from the doers, the achievers, the risk takers to be successful. If Big Brother would get his hand out of our pockets, we would provide more jobs and build more wealth. Theft is not right no matter what good name you put to it.

It is up to us to send as little to the shark as possible. One problem is that the so-called tax professionals are so intimidated by the long arm of the law. What is it—62%, 70%, 68% of the answers from government agents, tax preparers, and CPAs are wrong?

I'm an ex-cab driver. I study everything I can get my hands on. I make millions and want to be an expert on these matters. My seminars use proven strategies. Call my office for information on these topics. Especially get information (in my **Financial Fortress** set) about charitable remainder trusts. With this entity, you can save money now and give it to a charity (your church) later. It lets you seriously reduce your estate and inheritance taxes. It lets you live on the income. I particularly like the CRUT, or unit trust. I'm not fond of the CRAT, or annuity trust.

This is a powerful tool for controlling your wealth now, living your retirement, and semi-controlling your wealth after you're gone. There are too many legal strategies to list here. Study "Appendix C: Tax Structuring" to learn more about these opportunities to be good stewards.

I'll paraphrase Ronald Reagan. He said that if we want to be patriotic, quit sending so much to Washington. Keep your money at home beautifying your neighborhoods, creating jobs, et cetera. I choose to be patriotic in this way.

I want to tribute unto Caesar only what I legally have to, and make that tribute (tax) as small as possible. There are just too many other things to do for God with the wealth He gives us—without the middleman of government. We don't need our money taken and then used daily in hundreds of ways doing immoral things which violate God's ways and His plans.

Let's become students of the tax process. If we don't, more than necessary will be taken and used for these purposes. If you and I want our money used for good purposes, we'll have to find ways to keep more and then rely on inspiration for the use of it.

*We also . . . desire that ye might be
filled with the knowledge of His will in
all wisdom and spiritual understanding;
That ye might walk worthy
of the Lord unto all pleasing,
being fruitful in every good work,
and increasing in
the knowledge of God.
Colossians 1: 9, 10*

12

A Life Of Quality

There are certain characteristics of our individual lives which can be developed. This chapter is to point them out and give ways to strengthen the good qualities. God has much in store for us. We have to be more like Him if we want these things.

I've been in business a long time. I have had dealings with hundreds of producers, suppliers, promoters and contractors. I have lived and worked with over 500 people. I haven't seen it all, but darn close. I've had to fire people. I've been stolen from, embezzled from, lied to and betrayed. I, however, have no complaints. I have had inept officials look at my actions, and I have won and continue to win. When you're high profile like I have been, you rankle people. Ironically, my company is out to help investors against unscrupulous brokers and professionals and it's as if the very forces of nature rise up to prevent us from doing our good work.

The trials have made me what I am. Solving problems, trying new things, suffering and working with employees to find the really good ones, and battling every day to do good things and produce good results is one key to success.

If I have been guilty of anything it is that I won't give up. When we have questions, I'll do research, talk to many employees, ponder consequences with friends and then go to God for guidance.

In all this, I have had a strong wish to never say anything that I would have to apologize for. Simply, to be kind in all my dealings. God can forgive when He wants; it is my responsibility to forgive all. I still don't have to take bad things from people, but I can walk away from bad situations, choose carefully my battles and at all times try to walk uprightly. I fail sometimes and it is up to me to apologize, seek forgiveness and try harder. In short, I want the golden rule to be part of my guidance system:

> 12 **Therefore all things whatsoever ye would that men should do to you, do ye even so to them: for this is the law and the prophets.**
>
> **Matthew 7:12**

I feel no better advice can be given to help keep us close to God. Think of it. People have problems. You may be lied to; you may feel that giving $10 to the guy looking for food on the corner will go to drugs or alcohol (what is it—85% of the money goes to the harmful substances?); you may be wary of trying to help. It is still important to look on the heart, try to determine intent, judge righteously and then treat people like you would want to be treated.

All I've asked of my employees is the reverse of this—do this for the company: act in a way that you would like if this were your company:

> 22 **But the fruit of the Spirit is love, joy, peace, longsuffering, gentleness, goodness, faith.**
>
> **Galatians 5:22**

Grace

The word "grace" is used throughout the Bible. Paul uses it frequently referring to the awesome saving power of Jesus. It means "help or power to succor."

I'd like to use this last definition and a more modern usage of the word. Grace is all these things but it is also more in that we can apply these characteristics ourselves. "To be graceful," or, "to be gracious," is the usage I refer to.

Many people have just not learned how to be civil. Civility is so important in our dealings with others. If your career or your company handles problems in a graceful manner, everyone is so much the better.

The best example of this is my wife. I get all the limelight. When she ran the company, she was called upon to do the "down in the trenches" work. She is a peacemaker. She has class. People constantly tell me how gracious she is. She would never say anything hurtful or cutting to anyone. Oh, she teases me all the time, but even her easy sarcasm is classic. I have seen her in hundreds of situations and settings and never once has she embarrassed herself, me, or the Lord. She exemplifies Godlike virtues as her way of life.

I saw a bumper sticker this morning, "So many women, so few ladies." It was fortuitous as I was about to write this small section on grace. I want to publicly thank my wife and the other great ladies in my life: my mother, my mother-in-law, my two sisters and my sister who has passed, my sister-in-law, my nieces, my daughters, and the ladies I work with.

They are all classy. They are either gracious or are working on it. I think men can learn a lot by watching how the graceful ladies in their lives act in situations of stress and growth. Every company I know can learn to be more gracious. We need to develop this characteristic. Again, God has set the example. We need to follow His ways:

> 27 **And it shall come to pass, when he crieth unto me, that I will hear: for I am gracious.**
>
> **Exodus 22:27**

Steadfastness

Replete in the scriptures is the admonition to remain steadfast. What an interesting attribute. Obviously most references are to things of a spiritual nature. There are, however, references to remaining firm:

11 Not slothful in business; fervent in spirit; serving the Lord.

Romans 12:11

11 And that ye study to be quiet, and to do your own business, and to work with your own hands, as we commanded you;

12 That ye may walk honestly toward them that are without, and that ye may have lack of nothing.

1 Thessalonians 4:11-12

Again, business is our personal endeavors. But here in Thessalonians, it is quite clear this usage refers to making a living. Note also once again, the reference to others. Hardly a scriptural thought goes by without being brought to a remembrance of our need to love and serve others. It's not odd when you think of it. Christ, Himself, was steadfast in His mission. He gave it His all for the benefit of others and while we are not asked to do what He did, we still must be willing to share and care for others.

Think of the opposite of this. Can you imagine God, who wants us to live well but also to endure all things, being happy with us if we shirk our duties, or are lax in our responsibilities? No, He won't be happy if we do wrong things. We must take care of our families and prepare for them. To not do so would be less than an "infidel."

What righteous laws can we be steadfast in? Here is a partial list:

- Steadfast in our learning of the word of God.
- Steadfast in our devotion to serve.

- Steadfast in our desire to employ wisdom and make wise choices.
- Steadfast in our resolve to do many good things on our own accord.
- Steadfast to see the big picture and not get caught up in the moment.
- Steadfast in our patience and longsuffering towards others.
- Steadfast in kindness and speaking well of others.
- Steadfast in our abhorrence of rumors, backbiting.
- Steadfast in our dedication to truth telling and honesty in all things.
- Steadfast to the covenant of Abraham, and staying within it.
- Steadfast in our prayers, our concerns, and our doing the will of God.

It is so easy to start (projects, businesses, activities), but so tough to finish. So much in life comes down to our resolve. Very seldom does a committee, or group, or business have the resolve to finish and succeed.

Almost every major accomplishment in the history of mankind has come from the resolve, the vision, and the mission of one man or woman. From Noah to Abraham, from Isaiah to Malachi. Even the list of Caesars. There is one Ben Franklin, one George Washington, one Thomas Jefferson, one Abraham Lincoln, one Ronald Reagan. There is one Marie Curie, one Louis Pasteur, one Jonas Salk. The point, my friends, is that in your own life, in your family, you are the one and of you much is expected. Great things are needed by those endowed with blessings from on high.

You are "sine qua non" to your successful life. No one can choose a proxy—someone to succeed for them. You can have friends, I hope you're blessed with many; you can have talents and abilities, which I hope will strengthen and become perfected as you use them; you can have wealth, which I know God will provide as you walk uprightly in the covenant;

but as you proceed, there is one fact that is certain: you need to be dedicated to God's cause. Great people do great things. Your steadfastness will help you finish all you set out to do.

Forgiving: The Sabbatical Year

I was busy a few years ago studying the Year of Jubilee. It was a 50th year celebration of feasts, worship and specific events — including particular things God's people were to do.

This led me to information on the Sabbatical Year. This particular custom was celebrated every seventh year in remembrance of all the great things God has done for us. I'm convinced God wants to be remembered and when He walks into our life, He leaves tracks. He sets in motion awesome parts of nature to help us remember Him. He causes a friend's comment, a story, a song, a scripture to be indelibly etched in our mind. He wants to be first.

So much good has come to my family from what I'm about to write. I hope it also will be helpful to you.

In the Sabbatical Year, one was to forgive the debts owed him. There were many other things to be done. It is the year of the Sabbath. It is time to give back to the Lord on His terms. Maybe it's like this: With our money (flocks, harvest, income) He wants one-tenth as a tithe, but with our time (our mind) He wants one-seventh. Just a thought. Anyway, the Sabbath is important to God. It is His day.

This year is important to God. It is His year to help set us straight. To correct problems; to learn to be one with each other so we can draw closer to Him. The Year of the Sabbath —it has a nice ring to it.

If I wanted to live this ancient principle, where would I start? An overwhelming feeling came over me. I felt I was being led along. It just so happened that year was my four-teenth wedding anniversary. Fourteen is two sets of seven. This could be my own Sabbatical Year. I went to my wife with a plan. She readily accepted it. We could not do all of the things they did in ancient Israel, but we could forgive debts.

We had loaned money to various people: $2,000 here, $8,000 there, $10,000 for a car, and $6,000 for whatever. I used to joke in my seminars that I loaned a friend $8,000 for plastic surgery and now I can't find him. These loans were not being repaid. They were causing bad feelings. Not on my part, but good friends quit coming to visit. I didn't like these feelings and was already starting to be so blessed in material things.

My wife and I wrote each of these people a letter. It explained what we knew of the Law of the Sabbatical Year. We would do away with the debt. They would hear no more about it from us. If they wanted to repay it later, that was up to them, but from our point of view, it was forgiven—gone.

I'm sure when they received this letter they thought they would get a chewing out, or a demand for payment. Each has thanked us with tearful words.

It's time to get on and put things behind us. How much baggage can we carry and still seek God diligently? This experience has been part of our cleansing process. It has taken a weight off of us—as the Lender.

I know it is a true principle—it is wisdom from the ancients that brings much good in the present. Our blessings increased.

Patience

2 My brethren, count it all joy when ye fall into divers temptations;
3 Knowing this, that the trying of your faith worketh patience.
4 But let patience have her perfect work, that ye may be perfect and entire, wanting nothing.

James 1:2-4

This is a difficult section for me to write because I like to get things done—I like to see results. There is an ancient Japanese proverb which says, "Tenbatsu wa Tekimen." "Tenbatsu" is punishment, or more precisely, Heaven penalty. "Tekimen," is rapid or quickly. The best English translation would be, "swift is Heaven's vengeance."

I know in spiritual things God will try us with fire. He wants to forge us into what He knows we can become. Patience through this process is a virtue indeed.

In financial matters the process is just as long. For example: I have worked for 17 years—doing seminars, producing home study courses, writing books, and traveling to every nook and cranny in this country. I have been in front of hundreds of thousands of people. I have been on over 1,600 radio and TV talk shows. I have written over 20 books. After all this, this last year I finally got a book on the *New York Times* Business Best Sellers List. Seventeen years of working diligently and now I'm an overnight success.

My tenacity, persistence, and patience would have carried me longer if needed. I believe in God. I believe He is true to His word. Recently I read a book about the Bible that said wealth is a gift, not a reward. The author said a reward would make it like "trading." I agree in a way, but look at the following verse:

> 6 **But without faith it is impossible to please Him: for he that cometh to God must believe that He is, and that He is a rewarder of them that diligently seek Him.**
>
> **Hebrews 11:6**

Yes, wealth, riches, other virtues, and eternal life are gifts, but often given as we seek and follow Him. Patience is necessary. Added to hope and much prayer, it will help see us through. Read on:

> 35 **Cast not away therefore your confidence, which hath great recompense of reward.**

36 For ye have need of patience, that, after ye
   have done the will of God, ye might receive
   the promise.

37 For yet a little while, and he that shall come
   will come, and will not tarry.

38 Now the just shall live by faith: but if any man
   draw back, my soul shall have no pleasure in
   him.

39 But we are not of them who draw back unto
   perdition; but of them that believe to the
   saving of the soul.

1 Now faith is the substance of things hoped
   for, the evidence of things not seen.

Hebrew 10:35-39, 11:1

Talk about things not seen. God's patience with me must run thin sometimes. I have a tendency to brag. Let me tell you of almost a daily occurrence. I drive a lot. I consider myself a good driver, but I've had to get a car with wood trim interior because I need something to knock on so often. Somebody pulls out in front of me, I check the mirrors, swerve and miss an accident in a talented way. Just as I'm about to gloat, bam—a curb pops up, and "that something unseen" gets in the way of my tire.

Seriously, I can hardly feel good about anything (being overly proud) until my humility is brought back into play. I'm sure we all need to work on patience; in our relationships, our material life, and our spiritual life:

18 And therefore will the Lord wait, that He may
   be gracious unto you, and therefore will He
   be exalted, that He may have mercy upon you:
   for the Lord is a God of judgment: blessed
   are all they that wait for Him.

Isaiah 30:18

Might

Dr. Orison Swett Marden, founded *Success* magazine in the late 1890s; nigh on one hundred years ago. I have read the magazine for years. It is well thought out and over the years has given much good help to so many people. I commend you to this wonderful magazine.

Dr. Marden was heavily influenced by a book which was quite popular throughout the world. It was called *Self Help*, first published in 1859. The author was a "Great Scot," Samuel Smiles. He often quoted the scriptural injunction, "Whatsoever thy hand findeth to do, do it with thy might; for there is no work, nor device, nor knowledge, nor wisdom, in the grave, whither thou goest." (Ecclesiastes 9:10) Not someone else's borrowed might or energy. Not halfheartedly, but with your might. Another scriptural injunction is this: do all that you do heartily:

> 23 **And whatsoever ye do, do it heartily, as to the Lord, and not unto men.**
>
> **Colossians 3:23**

Powerful advice, but so few get it. Mediocrity seems to reign supreme. No wonder that excellent people and excellent companies stick out. The difference, usually, between a good business and a poor business is very small. Likewise the difference between a good business and a great business is not large, but small—maybe even a few extra sales per day or per week. It is the little extra "second mile" things that make big differences. Lately, I've been impressed by certain singers, certain athletes, and even certain politicians: Why them? Because they're so visible, but my point is that the intense ones stick out. They give it their all. They dig in and their enthusiasm, their passion sticks out. They are different and the world knows it. Noah was different. He stuck out. He was ridiculed. Jesus definitely stuck out. Even His family wanted Him to tone it down. If you want to be extraordinary, and choose not to be ordinary—or do extraordinary (non-conventional) things or perform in innovative or creative ways—then your sticking out will attract attention.

Most people are lukewarm. They have no passion. I ask my children questions of choice. Do you want to go to McDonalds? If they reply, "I don't care," I drive on by. "Hey, I thought we were going to McDonald's." "No," I reply, "you said you didn't care." I won't accept "I don't care" as an answer. Make up your mind. An "I don't care" attitude doesn't get you anywhere.

In business, make up your mind. Gather information. Do a thorough job. Ponder, meditate, pray, and then make a decision; implement your choice and do it heartily. If it was a mistake, change and start over. But do it with passion.

I've mentioned on several radio interviews, that I want to live my life in the second mile—to be a second mile person. This is almost always met with more questions. What does it mean? Remember the statement: "And whosoever shall compel thee to go a mile, go with him twain?" (Matthew 5:41) "And if any man will sue thee at the law, and take away thy coat, let him have thy cloke also?" (Matthew 5:40) This is how I want to live. Most people who want to achieve excellence either learn this by reading or by watching other people, or by personal experience. The second mile is where so much good happens—where excellence is achieved—and, most importantly, where we'll find happiness.

You know when you're there in the second mile. You can feel it when you've gone the extra mile, or performed extra things. You'll know you've put in an honest day's work or more than an honest day's work. You'll go home satisfied—content with your work, and content with your reward.

To me, it seems the Lord doesn't want people who do just enough to get by. The world is full of such. Remember :

15 **I know thy works, that thou art neither cold nor hot: I would thou wert cold or hot.**
16 **So then because thou art lukewarm, and neither cold nor hot, I will spue thee out of my mouth.**

Revelation 3:15-16

Samuel Smiles said: "Success is found in helping and stimulating men to elevate and improve themselves by their own fire and independent individual action. The invisible world is all about us. The invisible world about is packed with infinite possibilities, awaiting our thought seed, our desire seed, our ambition seed, our prosperity and success seed."

What about our mustard seed?

Serenity

I'm writing this part for myself. Maybe someone else needs more serenity and peace in their life, I sure know I do.

If we take our burdens to the Lord and take upon us His load, we will be so much better off:

> 28 Come unto me, all ye that labor and are heavy laden, and I will give you rest.
> 29 Take my yoke upon you, and learn of me; for I am meek and lowly in heart: and ye shall find rest unto your souls.
> 30 For my yoke is easy, and my burden is light.

Matthew 11:28-30

Business endeavors are not conducive to quietness. But it is this step which needs to be taken:

> 10 Be still, and know that I am God: I will be exalted among the heathen, I will be exalted in the earth.

Psalms 46:10

Awhile back, I was in San Diego, a most beautiful city. I was way out (two blocks or so) on a rock jetty. I was so far out I could look back and see the back side of the waves. Here I was, once again, away from home. I felt I had to do everything to do well. I was way too busy.

I saw a pelican floating there. Once in a while it would dip its head in the water—the moving waves. I thought of the clams, the shrimp, and all those creepy things and realized God provides. It stayed put, and (to a certain extent) the ocean brings it what it needs.

I needed faith to do less. It was one of those stepping stones—so necessary to reaching the top. Now I take time out to ponder, to meditate, to read good books. Things are going so much better since I quit trying so hard.

Ultimately, we seek eternal peace. It can be hard to find in this world. We need to take time to build habits of serenity.

Out of Our Mouths

11 A word fitly spoken is like apples of gold in pictures of silver.

Proverbs 25:11

Words are powerful. God shows us His desires toward us by His words; we should show God our attitude toward Him by our words:

34 O generation of vipers, how can ye, being evil, speak good things? for out of the abundance of the heart the mouth speaketh.
35 A good man out of the good treasure of the heart bringeth forth good things: and an evil man out of the evil treasure bringeth forth evil things.
36 But I say unto you, That every idle word that men shall speak, they shall give account thereof in the day of judgment.
37 For by thy words thou shalt be justified, and by thy words thou shalt be condemned.

Matthew 12:34-37

We need to speak good words out loud. It is our words which show so much. Remember, it's not what we take into our bellies but what comes out of our mouths which condemns them. Likewise, the opposite is true. If what comes out of our mouth is praiseworthy, good, faithful and reverent, then God knows how we feel and will take action.

Listen to what He said to Daniel:

12   Then said He unto me, Fear not, Daniel: for from the first day that thou didst set thine heart to understand, and to chasten thyself before thy God, thy words were heard, and I am come for thy words.

Daniel 10:12

He will come for His words. Think of this. We, like Daniel, need to say the right words through faith. Let's be careful to speak correctly to each other. We don't need bad words. We need pleasant, thankful words of understanding. Our words trickle through our organization of business and church. Let's make sure our words are on God's side so He can do the following:

5   Who satisfieth thy mouth with good things; so that thy youth is renewed like the eagle's.

Psalms 103:5

How To "Be"

I give you one last grouping of scriptures which are so beautiful:

1   And seeing the multitudes, He went up into a mountain: and when He was set, His disciples came unto Him:

2   And He opened His mouth, and taught them, saying,

3   Blessed are the poor in spirit: for theirs is the kingdom of heaven.

4   Blessed are they that mourn: for they shall be comforted.

5   Blessed are the meek: for they shall inherit the earth.

6   Blessed are they which do hunger and thirst after righteousness: for they shall be filled.

7   Blessed are the merciful: for they shall obtain mercy.

8   Blessed are the pure in heart: for they shall see God.

9   Blessed are the peacemakers: for they shall be called the children of God.

10   Blessed are they which are persecuted for righteousness' sake: for theirs is the kingdom of heaven.

11   Blessed are ye, when men shall revile you, and persecute you, and shall say all manner of evil against you falsely, for my sake.

12   Rejoice, and be exceeding glad: for great is your reward in heaven: for so persecuted they the prophets which were before you.

Matthew 5:1-12

13

*Set your affection on things above,
not on things on earth.
Colossians 3:2*

Do's And Don'ts

10 Create in me a clean heart, O God; and renew
a right spirit within me.
11 Cast me not away from Thy presence; and take
not Thy holy spirit from me.
12 Restore unto me the joy of Thy salvation; and
uphold me with Thy free spirit.

Psalms 51:10-12

Success financially—is it possible? What will help, what
will hinder? The following are disparate scriptures which
are more "thou shalts" and "thou shalt nots." I've put the "thou
shalt nots" up front. You'll note very little commentary as
these are wonderful verses and need no explanation—only
a tie between them:

4 Ye adulterers and adulteresses, know ye not
that the friendship of the world is enmity with
God? Whosoever therefore will be a friend of
the world is the enemy of God.

James 4:4

We cannot be a renegade to God's plan. We need His word,
His gospel, to tame us. Just like a wild beast cannot tame
itself, so we need to be tamed by a loving God:

28 He that hath no rule over his own spirit is like a city that is broken down, and without walls.

Proverbs 25:28

We must cease to be vain:

11 Wealth gotten by vanity shall be diminished: but he that gathereth by labour shall increase.

Proverbs 13:11

We have to shun sin, overcome temptation, and cease to be wicked:

6 In the house of the righteous is much treasure: but in the revenues of the wicked is trouble.

Proverbs 15:6

When it comes to wealth we cannot love it for its own sake. It will perish. We need to only seek satisfaction from doing His work:

10 He that loveth silver shall not be satisfied with silver; nor he that loveth abundance with increase: this is also vanity.

Ecclesiastes 5:10

As I've said elsewhere, it seems that wealth gets us—not us it. Labour to love God and others. Do these first and then other things will be added to you:

4 Labour not to be rich: cease from thine own wisdom.

Proverbs 23:4

Following is story is told of Dives and Lazarus. Read it. Ponder it. There is a wealth of information here:

19 There was a certain rich man, which was clothed in purple and fine linen, and fared sumptuously every day:

20 And there was a certain beggar named Lazarus, which was laid at his gate, full of sores,

21 And desiring to be fed with the crumbs which fell from the rich man's table: moreover the dogs came and licked his sores.

22 And it came to pass, that the beggar died, and was carried by the angels into Abraham's bosom: the rich man also died, and was buried;

23 And in hell he lift up his eyes, being in torments, and seeth Abraham afar off, and Lazarus in his bosom.

24 And he cried and said, Father Abraham, have mercy on me, and send Lazarus, that he may dip the tip of his finger in water, and cool my tongue; for I am tormented in this flame.

25 But Abraham said, Son, remember that thou in thy lifetime receivedst thy good things, and likewise Lazarus evil things: but now he is comforted, and thou art tormented.

Luke 16:19-25

We can't be deluded by wealth:

4 Wealth maketh many friends; but the poor is separated from his neighbour.

Proverbs 19:4

It is so easy to get caught up in the ways of the world. Temptation and distractions are everywhere:

2 And be not conformed to this world: but be ye transformed by the renewing of your mind, that ye may prove what is that good, and acceptable, and perfect, will of God.

Romans 12:2

If we do get caught up in the world a mighty battle will ensue. It is hard to justify the things of God to a coveting, lustful attitude:

16 **This I say then, Walk in the Spirit, and ye shall not fulfil the lust of the flesh.**

17 **For the flesh lusteth against the Spirit, and the Spirit against the flesh: and these are contrary the one to the other: so that ye cannot do the things that ye would.**

Galatians 5:16-17

One thing to be sure of is not to fall into coveting:

15 **And He said unto them, Take heed, and beware of covetousness: for a man's life consisteth not in the abundance of the things which he possesseth.**

Luke 12:15

We have to watch how we embrace worldly pleasures:

9 **Thou hast loved righteousness, and hated iniquity; therefore God, even thy God, hath anointed thee with the oil of gladness above thy fellows.**

Hebrew 1:9

And now we come to many "thou shalts"—things we can do. This list is by no means all inclusive. There are many, many more to be found. Just as John asks:

28 **Then said they unto Him, What shall we do, that we might work the works of God?**

John 6:28

34 **Wait on the Lord, and keep His way, and He shall exalt thee to inherit the land: when the wicked are cut off, thou shalt see it.**

Psalms 37:34

I find the following phrase most interesting:

14 **Then shalt thou delight thyself in the Lord; and I will cause thee to ride upon the high places of the earth, and feed thee with the heritage of Jacob thy father: for the mouth of the Lord hath spoken it.**

Isaiah 58:14

He is not hard to follow. Following the ways of the world — that is hard. His ways are delightful if we seek Him joyfully. Our delight grows *as* we continue.

In the next verse we find the word "lack" once again. A clear cut answer on how to avoid it, " seek the Lord":

10 **The young lions do lack, and suffer hunger: but they that seek the Lord shall not want any good thing.**

Psalms 34:10

We cannot seek the Lord if we continue in sin. Something has to give. Something has to change:

7 **Let the wicked forsake his way, and the unrighteous man his thoughts: and let him return unto the Lord, and He will have mercy upon him; and to our God, for He will abundantly pardon.**

Isaiah 55:7

I rejoice that He will abundantly pardon. And how do we get to this point? How do we keep our head on straight? It's a matter of attitude. Isaiah has a great answer:

19 **If ye be willing and obedient, ye shall eat the good of the land:**
20 **But if ye refuse and rebel, ye shall be devoured with the sword: for the mouth of the Lord hath spoken it.**

Isaiah 1:19-20

I'm intrigued every time I come across scriptures with the words "good fruits" or "bring forth fruits." Those that have faith <u>and</u> do the works will bear good fruits:

> 20 **And these are they which are sown on good ground; such as hear the word, and receive it, and bring forth fruit, some thirtyfold, some sixty, and some an hundred.**
>
> **Mark 4:20**

And where do we learn the word and how to apply it? Read this verse:

> 8 **This book of the law shall not depart out of thy mouth; but thou shalt meditate therein day and night, that thou mayest observe to do according to all that is written therein: for then thou shalt make thy way prosperous, and then thou shalt have good success.**
>
> **Joshua 1:8**

I know I've used this verse before but I just think it is powerful. Its challenge is "observe and do," and look what happens if we are faithful to this course. He has so much in store for us here:

> 19 **If ye be willing and obedient, ye shall eat the good of the land.**
>
> **Isaiah 1:19**

> 8 **And God is able to make all grace abound toward you; that ye, always having all sufficiency in all things, may abound to every good work:**
> 9 **(As it is written, He hath dispersed abroad; He hath given to the poor: His righteousness remaineth for ever.**
> 10 **Now He that ministereth seed to the sower both minister bread for your food, and multiply your seed sown, and increase the fruits of your righteousness;)**

11 Being enriched in every thing to all bountifulness, which causeth through us thanksgiving to God.

2 Corinthians 9:8-11

Grace now and in the world to come. We have many things to do. We must work:

2 For thou shalt eat the labour of thine hands: happy shalt thou be, and it shall be well with thee.

Psalms 128:2

We must rest on the Sabbath:

9 Six days shalt thou labour, and do all thy work:
10 But the seventh day is the sabbath of the Lord thy God: in it thou shalt not do any work, thou, nor thy son, nor thy daughter, thy manservant, nor thy maidservant, nor thy cattle, nor thy stranger that is within thy gates.

Exodus 20:9-10

We must be diligent in all our endeavors:

11 And that ye study to be quiet, and to do your own business, and to work with your own hands, as we commanded you.

1 Thessalonians 4:11

If not, we are not to eat:

10 For even when we were with you, this we commanded you, that if any would not work, neither should he eat.

2 Thessalonians 3:10

Note: Big Brother, please read this.

We need the gains God promises. Being content is a big part of this:

> 6 But godliness with contentment is great gain.
> 7 For we brought nothing into this world, and it is certain we can carry nothing out.
> 8 And having food and raiment let us be therewith content.
>
> 1 Timothy 6:6-8

And why be anxious any way?

> 28 And why take ye thought for raiment? Consider the lilies of the field, how they grow; they toil not, neither do they spin.
>
> Matthew 6:28

All He has awaits us:

> 32 Fear not, little flock; for it is your Father's good pleasure to give you the kingdom.
>
> Luke 12:32

We must resist temptation:

> 12 Blessed is the man that endureth temptation: for when he is tried, he shall receive the crown of life, which the Lord hath promised to them that love him.
>
> James 1:12

Again, one area to avoid temptation is the enticements of the world:

> 14 But every man is tempted, when he is drawn away of his own lust, and enticed.
>
> James 1:14

If we do err, let's be quick to repent. Let's be quick to accept the chastisement of God:

12 Blessed is the man whom Thou chastenest, O Lord, and teachest him out of Thy law;
13 That thou mayest give him rest from the days of adversity, until the pit be digged for the wicked.

Psalms 94:12-13

He will help us:

10 Finally, my brethren, be strong in the Lord, and in the power of His might.
11 Put on the whole armour of God, that ye may be able to stand against the wiles of the devil.
12 For we wrestle not against flesh and blood, but against principalities, against powers, against the rulers of the darkness of this world, against spiritual wickedness in high places.
13 Wherefore take unto you the whole armour of God, that ye may be able to withstand in the evil day, and having done all, to stand.
14 Stand therefore, having your loins girt about with truth, and having on the breastplate of righteousness.

Ephesians 6:10-14

Yes, we must work:

23 In all labour there is profit: but the talk of the lips tendeth only to penury.

Proverbs 14:23

His admonition is simple:

2 Keep My commandments, and live; and My law as the apple of thine eye.

Proverbs 7:2

One commandment is to love one another. Express our love by serving—by doing something:

> 13 For, brethren, ye have been called unto liberty; only use not liberty for an occasion to the flesh, but by love serve one another.
>
> Galatians 5:13

> 26 But it shall not be so among you: but whosoever will be great among you, let him be your minister;
> 27 And whosoever will be chief among you, let him be your servant.
>
> Matthew 20:26-27

The greatest commandment is to love God. If we love Him and seek Him we shall find Him:

> 17 I love them that love Me; and those that seek Me early shall find Me.
>
> Proverbs 8:17

To do so we must seek His eternal treasures:

> 21 For where your treasure is, there will your heart be also.
>
> Matthew 6:21

He wants to prosper us:

> 27 Let them shout for joy, and be glad, that favour my righteous cause: yea, let them say continually, Let the Lord be magnified, which hath pleasure in the prosperity of His servant.
>
> Psalms 35:27

But, of course, we have to act. To do much good:

> 22 But be ye doers of the word, and not hearers only, deceiving your own selves.
>
> James 1:22

When all is said and done, when we've searched for our own souls, our mission in life—when we've spent endless hours pondering those deeper things and come up wondering where the answers are and who will help us—at this time I leave you this last verse:

31 **What shall we then say to these things? If God be for us, who can be against us?**

Romans 8:31

Whatsoever things are true,
whatsoever things are honest,
whatsoever things are just,
whatsoever things are pure,
whatsoever things are lovely,
whatsoever things are of good report;
if there be any virtue,
and if there be any praise,
think on these things.
Philippians 4:8

14

A Month Of Good Things

Here is a month of good things to do. Read one every day. Implement the principle. Put it to work. You'll notice that I left every seventh day for something to do with the Sabbath.

Day 1: Giving And Taking

In another place I quoted the scripture about not having diverse weights and measures. In this scripture out of Luke, we have a variation of the words, but even a more powerful lesson is taught:

> 38 Give, and it shall be given unto you; good measure, pressed down, and shaken together, and running over, shall men give into your bosom. For with the same measure that ye mete withal it shall be measured to you again.
>
> **Luke 6:38**

How we treat people is how we'll be treated. Let me say it another way. Let's say an employee comes to a company and really likes the boss. The employee acts nice to the boss. Kind words are spoken, diligent work is performed, et cetera. The boss's opinion of the employee will probably come to resemble the employee's opinion of the boss. Conversely, if you really dislike someone, their opinion of you will more than likely come to resemble your opinion of them. God has His own law of the harvest. In relationships, in dealing with others, we should take care to give and to measure out of the goodness of our hearts.

Day 2: Sowing And Reaping

We reap what we sow. If you're over eight years old, you already should have figured this principle out—at least to a certain extent. Studying a certain amount of time, or with varying effectiveness, produces different grades. Study well and get "A's." Be less than diligent, then you get "B's" and "C's." If you practice the piano or play basketball, there is usually a direct relationship between the practice that you put in and the results. If you garden, you know you don't plant beans and get cauliflower.

Why then is it so hard to apply this to our spiritual lives? If you want God to be in your life and if developing your spiritual talents is important and needed so you can be more spiritual and grow and receive more of this type of blessings, then do what it takes. You don't gain a spiritual insight into, say, giving to others unless you live the principle. Only then does it become real. Then, as you sow, so you shall reap. Reread day one. It will be meted out to you.

All throughout the Bible you'll find references to "good fruits." Whether you want it or not, you will be known, even judged, by the fruits you bear. If you want good fruits, then plant good seeds, take care to water and nurse the plant and in time of harvest all will be well. You'll never get right results from wrong activities. You'll never achieve greatness by doing mediocre things:

> 23 **But he that received seed into the good ground is he that heareth the word, and understandeth it; which also beareth fruit, and bringeth forth, some an hundredfold, some sixty, some thirty.**
>
> **Matthew 13:23**

Day 3: Too Important?

Be careful what you think on and where you invest your time. Maybe something you think is so important it needs to be put in perspective. Is it making you anxious? Is it consuming you? We all live with stress. The farmer, with a seemingly simple life, has a ton of stress, but he learns to process things the right way.

Things need to be done in the proper order. Cross each bridge as you get to it. There is no sense planting the seeds until the earth is prepared. With each job, business, function, first figure out the process. Learn the rules. Then proceed. Prioritize the elements. If all you're doing is ultimately designed to build His kingdom, all will be well. If something becomes too important to you, you take your eye off the goal.

Day 4: Lending Money

Use a lot of discretion in your lending practices. I'm not one to advise to not lend money to your family members and friends, but I will say it has caused many heartaches for me. My wife was recently burned by friends in the horse business. It is hard to forget these things.

A good question to ask yourself, "Will this loan help or hinder the person?" Often, for them, borrowing is contrary to where they should be. Borrowing sometimes teaches wrong lessons.

The next question, "Is the loan properly documented with easy to understand terms?" Does everyone understand the contract? Also, are you lending to people who have bad repayment habits? Be careful.

The last question is, "Can your friendship withstand nonpayment?" The answer is usually not—at least for awhile. It's not because of you if you're the one lending the money, but because of the attitude of the borrower. If they can't repay, they'll quit calling, quit talking to you. In short, they will avoid you like the bank.

Again, use wisdom and discretion. In the Old Testament there is mention of not charging usury. Usury means interest. I've done research on this and this practice was for "my people," meaning God's people. You'll have to decide today how to deal with them. Usury also means an excessive interest charge (possibly illegal):

> 25 **If thou lend money to any of my people that is poor by thee, thou shalt not be to him as a usurer, neither shalt thou lay upon him usury.**
>
> Exodus 22:25

Day 5: Agree Quickly

A big part of my real estate seminars is showing people how to buy property the right way. Negotiating the best deal is so important. However, as important as negotiating is, I devised all kinds of strategies to help me avoid confrontational negotiating. Usually I would not negotiate at all. Just tell me what you want and it's yes or no. Even today I'm not thrilled about finagling over terms. I use the following verse in my seminars quite often:

> 25 **Agree with thine adversary quickly, whiles thou art in the way with him; lest at any time the adversary deliver thee to the judge, and the judge deliver thee to the officer, and thou be cast into prison.**
>
> Matthew 5:25

I used it to move the negativity along. Agree and then change the other terms, "Okay, you want $100,000, but if I give you your price will you consider taking $10,000 down?" This agreeing must happen now, "whiles thou art in the way." Keep reading the scripture and see other consequences. Don't take this scripture out of context, though. There was a specific reason for such treatment. We can avoid such anxiety and heartache caused by delay and uncertainty if we follow this advice.

Day 6: Make Good Music A Part Of Your Life

I used to be in a rock-n-roll band. I love good rock—with actual instruments and a heavy bass line. I also enjoy almost all other forms of music. Good music has passion. When I think back over the past few years, almost every moving spiritual experience I've had has been associated with music. A solo in church, a beautiful quartet on TV, "Amazing Grace" heard on bagpipes off in the distance at a 4th of July parade. I get more lumps in my throat by listening to good music than any other way. I love the songs of America. How great they are. It is not hard to access good music today. Cassette players, CDs—they are all so handy. If you want to fill up your life with sweet good things, music is a good ticket to providing the atmosphere:

> 16 **Let the word of Christ dwell in you richly in all wisdom; teaching and admonishing one another in Psalms and hymns and spiritual songs, singing with grace in your hearts to the Lord.**
>
> Colossians 3:16

Day 7: On the Seventh Day Rest

This is God's law. It makes sense spiritually, but it also makes sense physically. I know it's tough to avoid all worldly activities on the Sabbath, but we must try. Our bodies and minds need the rest. We live in a stressful society and economy. We need to wind down. More importantly, however, is the need to wind up spiritually. Attending church, hearing the Word, singing the hymns, and thinking on things of God. They are so important. Keep this day holy. Do you know the words holy, whole, and heal all stem from the same root word? This is, to many, the first day of the week. Peter, Paul, and James chose to celebrate this as the sabbath because it is the first day of the resurrection.

Day 8: Be Not Double Minded

Confusion will be eliminated when we set our lives in order toward God. All of us have a need to do this. One big step is to repent—to seek forgiveness. If we are to purify our hearts, we need to walk on righteous paths. We can't be hypocrites about this. We can't say one thing and do another. We may fool a few people for a short time, but not for long—and we will never fool God:

> 8 Draw nigh to God, and He will draw nigh to you. Cleanse your hands, ye sinners; and purify your hearts, ye doubleminded.
>
> **James 4:8**

If we are to purify our hearts we need to be people of integrity. Integrity means making what you think, what you say, what you do, even what you are, the same.

Day 9: Don't Be Busybodies

There is way too much rumor mongering and murmuring going on. It seems everyone gets caught up in the negative. One negative comment takes years to eradicate—possibly a bad rumor will never be corrected or beaten back. Stop such. If you run a company, don't be part of the small talk. When someone says, "Did you hear what so-and-so did?" Say, "I don't care to know. It's none of my business."

> 14 Forwardness is in his heart, he deviseth mischief continually; he soweth discord.
>
> **Proverbs 6:14**

Ask, "Will telling me this build up my sales, my business, or whatever? Will those comments help me, you or the person you want to talk about?" Nay saying is so easy:

> 12 A naughty person, a wicked man, walketh with a froward mouth.
>
> **Proverbs 6:12**

Being involved in petty, demeaning things seems to have replaced baseball as our national past time.

Day 10: *Live A Life Of Hope*

Hope for good things, hope for the blessings of Abraham's covenant to come to you. Hope in Christ—the rock of our salvation. The opposite of hope is despair. It serves no useful purpose. The only despair should be remorse over sin. Be on with it—repent and don't let it linger. Despair is Satan's workplace:

> 10 When Jesus had lifted up Himself, and saw none but the woman, He said unto her, Woman, where are those thine accusers? hath no man condemned thee?
>
> 11 She said, No man, Lord. And Jesus said unto her, Neither do I condemn thee: go, and sin no more.

John 8:10-11

Hope makes you feel young. Hope gives purpose to living. From hope springs many good things.

We all know really negative people. Most of us get tired of them. We need more optimism—more things to hope on. Think of it if that is our target—our "day to day" work out—our own salvation with fear and trembling—the peace that comes from righteous hope:

> 14 Wait on the Lord: be of good courage, and He shall strengthen thine heart: wait, I say, on the Lord.

Psalms 27:14

Day 11: *Tell the Truth*

Honesty is the best policy. Why? Because there is so little of it. Everywhere, at every level, people hide things, tell half truths, conceal real truths, even the facts. How wonderful it is to finally talk to someone who is completely open and honest.

Yes, sometimes tact is needed and sometimes (usually most of the time) certain truths about people are best not talked about. Kindness and "doing unto others" should be used. However when it's time to talk, do so with only the truth:

> 24 **Put away from thee a froward mouth, and perverse lips put far from thee.**
>
> **Proverbs 4:24**

Recently, we had to fire a person. He was inept and also stole from the company. Many talks and warnings were given to him. When his supervisor let him go, he hedged and blamed it on company cutbacks. That was not the truth. This person needs to know why he is no longer with us. Even if he disagrees—he needs to know our position. Usually, "brutal honesty" is necessary. There should be no misunderstandings:

> 3 **All the while my breath is in me, and the spirit of God is in my nostrils;**
> 4 **My lips shall not speak wickedness, nor my tongue utter deceit.**
>
> **Job 27:3-4**

Day 12: Riches Do Not Satisfy

The soul yearns for much more than a Mercedes can provide. We need the sweet communion with the Lord. Peace comes from believing and doing the word of God:

> 12 **The sleep of a labouring man is sweet, whether he eat little or much: but the abundance of the rich will not suffer him to sleep.**
>
> **Ecclesiastes 5:12**

Day 13: Don't Believe in Superstitions

Don't believe in stupid things of the world. 13 is not an unlucky number. If you concentrate on things of God you won't have time for such nonsense.

Avoid petty things. I teach someone how to take $5,000 and make $3,000 profit on a stock (or option) transaction. Invariably, I'll get the question, "But what about the $80 commission?" My retort, "Don't trip over pennies on your way to dollars." Likewise, don't trip over small, inconsequential sins on your way to Heaven. Think noble thoughts. God's ways are higher than worrying about black cats and broken mirrors.

Day 14:

The Sabbath is to be a physical day of rest. Why? So we can make it a spiritual day of wonders. You can't get the spirit of God into your life water skiing. Don't trade one kind of work for another. It is for resting. Use this day wisely—for God's purposes.

Day 15: No Excuses

Don't let excuses get in your way. As a business person you know how tired you are of excuses. That is one thing we Americans are good at—making excuses, passing the buck. The scripture says:

> 33 But seek ye first the kingdom of God, and His righteousness; and all these things shall be added unto you.
>
> Matthew 6:33

Don't let material things get in the way:

> 19 Lay not up for yourselves treasures upon earth, where moth and rust doth corrupt, and where thieves break through and steal.
>
> Matthew 6:19

Don't make excuses. Think how feeble they will sound at the end.

Day 16: The Mote And Beam

Awhile ago, I was really upset with someone at work for not putting something back exactly where they found it. It required me to change what I was doing, put the things I was carrying down, move the item back, pick up my stuff, and then proceed. It was so annoying.

I can't believe I'm even writing this. My anger was so petty. It's embarrassing to think back on how ticked off I was. I was just about to go find the person and vent my anger. I stopped. I wondered about myself. I wondered if God was in Heaven saying, "Darn that Wade Cook! Why can't he do exactly what I tell him to do?" I thought about this for quite some time. I even started to chuckle. God says:

1   Judge not, that ye be not judged.
2   For with what judgment ye judge, ye shall be judged: and with what measure ye mete, it shall be measured to you again.
3   And why beholdest thou the mote that is in thy brother's eye, but considerest not the beam that is in thine own eye?
4   Or how wilt thou say to thy brother, Let me pull out the mote out of thine eye; and, behold, a beam is in thine own eye?
5   Thou hypocrite, first cast out the beam out of thine own eye; and then shalt thou see clearly to cast out the mote out of thy brother's eye.

Matthew 7:1-5

A beam was in my eye. I was able later to calmly ask for it to be done right in the future.

Day 17: Give

You've heard the expression, "Something's got to give." It's true. When it comes to offerings, donations, gifts—true helping, whether money or energy—this expression takes on added meaning. Yes, someone's got to give. And if it's not you and me, who will it be?

Now I realize there is part of this expression which is left out. The "give" usually means "give way." Well, if we give many things, they will give way both to the giver and the receiver.

Day 18: Curb Your Anger

If we take seriously the Golden Rule, then we cannot in anger do that which is right. Anger will cause all the wrong emotions. It is a powerful tool used by Satan. When we get too wrapped up in our businesses, get too busy, find ourselves under too much stress, then we find ourselves getting mad over the smallest of things. How I wish I could take back all the things I've said when I was frustrated or angry. I can't, but I can keep trying to do all I can with patience and understanding.

I know it's cliche, but I've noticed that when people are wrong, they get angry. Their noise level is equal to their wrong level. Again, it is not God's way. If we want to be angry at sin or the Evil One, fine, but in other aspects curb your tongue, tone down the sarcasm, be enduringly patient.

Fathers should take heart to Colossians 3:21:"Fathers, provoke not your children to anger, lest they be discouraged." Fathers can hurt or help a family's situation so quickly. I'm appalled at the action of men today. Not all, but those who bully the weak, those who cause so much damage. Men, get a grip.

Anger simply will not solve problems. It will create problems, but cannot, by its very nature, bring people closer to God.

Day 19: Be Not Full Of Pride

Many words have multiple meanings. Pride is one of them. To be proud of one's quality work, or to diligently achieve a goal and to be singularly proud of this accomplishment, or to have pride in your children, surely is okay. When the pride turns to vanity and conceit then it turns sour. If you boast of your accomplishments, if you speak highly of yourself and disparage others, if you're consumed with your station in life then the Lord is displeased:

18 **Pride goeth before destruction, and a haughty spirit before a fall.**

Proverbs 16:18

Be grateful, be humble. Seek the best part. Put not your faith in things of this world. Remember that stupid bumper sticker, "He who dies with the most toys wins?" How naive. Wins what? You're still dead and your toys are being broken by people who didn't do anything to earn them. Recently I saw a T-shirt which said, "He who dies with the most toys is still dead. He who dies with God's gift lives forever."

Pride serves no useful purpose. It is detrimental to our growth. It takes us a few steps away from God. It shows that we only have faith in ourselves. Doing quality work, being a quality person is noticeable to God. We do this with humility:

2 **Every way of a man is right in his own eyes: but the Lord pondereth the hearts.**

Proverbs 21:2

Day 20: Thou Shalt Not Muzzle The Ox

If we have stewardship over animals, it is incumbent on us to take good care of them. I know the free cat given to us ends up costing $450 for an operation, I know the horse gets sick right when it's time for a vacation, I know the messes they make, but they are ours.

The scriptures say: "Thou shalt not muzzle the ox when he treadeth out the corn." (Deuteronomy 25:4) Even beasts of burden have a right to some grain on the threshing room floor. God's concern for all His creatures is endless.

Day 21: Remember The Sabbath

If this is your Sabbath, then simply read the following four verses. Let the spirit of God dictate to you how to keep this day holy:

8   Remember the sabbath day, to keep it holy.

9   Six days shalt thou labour, and do all thy work:

10 But the seventh day is the sabbath of the Lord thy God: in it thou shalt not do any work, thou, nor thy son, nor thy daughter, thy manservant, nor thy maidservant, nor thy cattle, nor thy stranger that is within thy gates:

11 For in six days the Lord made heaven and earth, the sea, and all that in them is, and rested the seventh day: wherefore the Lord blessed the sabbath day, and hallowed it.

Exodus 20:8-11

Day 22: Live The Ten Commandments

I'll list here the most common passage:

1   And God spake all these words, saying,

2   I am the Lord thy God, which have brought thee out of the land of Egypt, out of the house of bondage.

3   Thou shalt have no other gods before me.

4   Thou shalt not make unto thee any graven image, or any likeness of any thing that is in heaven above, or that is in the earth beneath, or that is in the water under the earth:

5 Thou shalt not bow down thyself to them, nor serve them: for I the Lord thy God am a jealous God, visiting the iniquity of the fathers upon the children unto the third and fourth generation of them that hate me;

6 And shewing mercy unto thousands of them that love me, and keep my commandments.

7 Thou shalt not take the name of the Lord thy God in vain; for the Lord will not hold him guiltless that taketh His name in vain.

8 Remember the sabbath day, to keep it holy.

9 Six days shalt thou labour, and do all thy work:

10 But the seventh day is the Sabbath of the Lord thy God: in it thou shalt not do any work, thou, nor thy son, nor thy daughter, thy manservant, nor thy maidservant, nor thy cattle, nor thy stranger that is within thy gates:

11 For in six days the Lord made heaven and earth, the sea, and all that in them is, and rested the seventh day: wherefore the Lord blessed the Sabbath day, and hallowed it.

12 Honour thy father and thy mother: that thy days may be long upon the land which the Lord thy God giveth thee.

13 Thou shalt not kill.

14 Thou shalt not commit adultery.

15 Thou shalt not steal.

16 Thou shalt not bear false witness against thy neighbour.

17 Thou shalt not covet thy neighbour's house, thou shalt not covet thy neighbour's wife, nor his manservant, nor his maidservant, nor his ox, nor his ass, nor any thing that is thy neighbour's.

Exodus 20:1-17

Day 23: Study The Ancient Laws

No book about the Bible could be complete without listing all the scriptures. There is no sense doing that as they are already in print. The first five books of the Bible, the Pentatuech, are full of God's laws, statutes, and commandments. Many financial laws are found in Leviticus and Deuteronomy and Proverbs. Many relationship laws are found through all five books, as well as throughout the other books.

I know this reading is sometimes tough going, but if we are to fill up our life with God and do this work, we must begin with His words. I realize much of this material deals with sacrifices and these don't apply to us today, but throughout these are powerful counsel and wonderful stories:

5   Ye shall therefore keep my statutes, and my judgments: which if a man do, he shall live in them: I am the Lord.

Leviticus 18:5

Day 24: Pray Often

Read the Lord's Prayer:

6   But thou, when thou prayest, enter into thy closet, and when thou hast shut thy door, pray to thy Father which is in secret; and thy Father which seeth in secret shall reward thee openly.

7   But when ye pray, use not vain repetitions, as the heathen do: for they think that they shall be heard for their much speaking.

8   Be not ye therefore like unto them: for your Father knoweth what things ye have need of, before ye ask Him.

9   After this manner therefore pray ye: Our Father which art in heaven, Hallowed be thy name.

10 Thy kingdom come. Thy will be done in earth,
as it is in heaven.

11 Give us this day our daily bread.

12 And forgive us our debts, as we forgive our
debtors.

13 And lead us not into temptation, but deliver
us from evil: For thine is the kingdom, and
the power, and the glory, for ever. Amen.

Matthew 6:6-13

Enter into a quiet place and pray. A prayer of thanksgiving, a prayer of praise, a prayer for help with relationships, a prayer for direction, and a prayer for inspiration. Quietly ask God to help you draw closer to Him. I know our schedules are busy, but what is more important than sweet communion with the God who made us? He who helps us, and who now has power to save us?

Day 25: Thou Shalt Not Tempt

This discussion will go two ways. The first: we should avoid getting ourselves into bad situations. The Evil One wants us. He will keep trying and will take us into sin any way he can. Here are some specific things which can be done daily:

- Don't get too tired. A tired body and mind is less strong against temptations.

- Respect others and look at their heart.

- Don't show off. We need humility.

- Don't flirt with others in the workplace or talk (tell dirty jokes) demeaningly.

- In the workplace, don't be alone with anyone of the opposite sex.

Let me tell you of our company policy. It is against our internal rules (we don't have many but the one's we do are very important) to be alone, even if it's a one-block ride to a restaurant for lunch, with someone of the opposite sex, even if you're single. Travel in groups. Even if a speaker and road crew travel to Chicago and the speaker (man) has to ride with the team leader (woman) to the seminar area, they are not to be alone. If there are three or four or more people then rent a car and go. If they need rental cars, then they rent one. But, if there is only one man and one woman, one must ride in a cab.

I don't want a wife back home having to worry about a company policy that encourages people (her husband) to be with other women in potentially harmful situations. I know this sounds petty, as they should be trusted. I do trust them when they're apart. But I don't want to introduce temptation. The eleventh commandment should be, "Thou shalt not tempt." I would rather be criticized for this and similar policies than have a family break up because of a short romantic interval that could have been prevented.

Actually, my employees enjoy this policy. They don't have to question what to do, or feel uncomfortable being alone with someone. They know the company will pay the extra $40 cab fare. Let me give you some more suggestions.

- Don't take even one paper clip from your company.
- Work an honest amount of time. If you work eight hours a day and you spend 15 minutes on a personal phone call, turn in seven hours and 45 minutes.
- Don't waste other people's time.
- Don't be idle—talk to your supervisor—he's ready to give you more to do.
- Always do more than you're asked: "And whosoever shall compel thee to go a mile, go with him twain." (Matthew 5: avoid temptation, but be strong and faithful when faced with such.

Day 26: Gold and Silver Have I None

I love Peter's statement when he met the lame man. Here was a man asking for money, a beggar. Peter didn't have what he wanted, but he did have what he needed. He had something all of us need. Listen to the power of his words:

1 Now Peter and John went up together into the temple at the hour of prayer, being the ninth hour.

2 And a certain man lame from his mother's womb was carried, whom they laid daily at the gate of the temple which is called Beautiful, to ask alms of them that entered into the temple;

3 Who seeing Peter and John about to go into the temple asked an alms.

4 And Peter, fastening his eyes upon him with John, said, Look on us.

5 And he gave heed unto them, expecting to receive something of them.

6 Then Peter said, Silver and gold have I none; but such as I have give I thee: In the name of Jesus Christ of Nazareth rise up and walk.

7 And he took him by the right hand, and lifted him up: and immediately his feet and ankle bones received strength.

8 And he leaping up stood, and walked, and entered with them into the temple, walking, and leaping, and praising God.

9 And all the people saw him walking and praising God:

10 And they knew that it was he which sat for alms at the Beautiful gate of the temple: and they were filled with wonder and amazement at that which had happened unto him.

11 And as the lame man which was healed held Peter and John, all the people ran together unto them in the porch that is called Solomon's, greatly wondering.

12 And when Peter saw it, he answered unto the people, Ye men of Israel, why marvel ye at this? or why look ye so earnestly on us, as though by our own power or holiness we had made this man to walk?

13 The God of Abraham, and of Isaac, and of Jacob, the God of our fathers, hath glorified His Son Jesus; whom ye delivered up, and denied Him in the presence of Pilate, when he was determined to let Him go.

14 But ye denied the Holy One and the Just, and desired a murderer to be granted unto you;

15 And killed the Prince of Life, whom God hath raised from the dead; whereof we are witnesses.

16 And His name through faith in His name hath made this man strong, whom ye see and know: yea, the faith which is by Him hath given him this perfect soundness in the presence of you all.

Acts 3:1-16

There are wonderful lessons here. One is that God will heal, and make us holy. I love Peter's answer, "Silver and gold have I none, but such as I have, give I thee." We all confront people who need more than we materially have to give. Sometimes they need faith, a kind word. They need healing and we should be ready to give what we can. God will inspire us by His spirit to know what to give.

Day 27: The Eleventh Hour

In the chapter after the one wherein the Lord dealt with young rich men is another wonderful story and parable:

1 For the kingdom of heaven is like unto a man that is an householder, which went out early in the morning to hire labourers into his vineyard.

2   And when he had agreed with the labourers for a penny a day, he sent them into his vineyard.

3   And he went out about the third hour,

4   And saw others standing idle in the marketplace, and said unto them; Go ye also into the vineyard, and whatsoever is right I will give you. And they went their way.

5   Again he went out about the sixth and ninth hour, and did likewise.

6   And about the eleventh hour he went out, and found others standing idle, and saith unto them, Why stand ye here all the day idle?

7   They say unto him, Because no man hath hired us. He saith unto them, Go ye also into the vineyard; and whatsoever is right, that shall ye receive.

8   So when even was come, the lord of the vineyard saith unto his steward, Call the labourers, and give them their hire, beginning from the last unto the first.

9   And when they came that were hired about the eleventh hour, they received every man a penny.

10 But when the first came, they supposed that they should have received more; and they likewise received every man a penny.

11 And when they had received it, they murmured against the goodman of the house,

12 Saying, These last have wrought but one hour, and thou hast made them equal unto us, which have borne the burden and heat of the day.

13 But he answered one of them, and said, Friend, I do thee no wrong: didst not thou agree with me for a penny?

14 Take that thine is, and go thy way: I will give unto this last, even as unto thee.

15 Is it not lawful for me to do what I will with mine own? Is thine eye evil, because I am good?

16 So the last shall be first, and the first last: for many be called, but few chosen.

Matthew 20:1-16

I love this story so much. It does not need my interpretation to be understood. I will only make a few comments. The householder went out to find laborers. He went out again and found others in the marketplace "standing idle." How true it is everywhere. He went again near to the eleventh hour and there were still some standing idle. He sent them into the vineyard. They could have gone by themselves. Work is everywhere. You can make work.

I used to own a small restaurant. One day a 20-year old boy (man) showed up and cleaned the whole outside of the property. I saw him and was so busy with other things I couldn't talk to him until after we opened. I thought the assistant manager had hired him. He came in after almost three hours, asked for me, and thanked me for allowing him to work. I said, "You're welcome. Is this all that Daryl gave you to do?" He said, "Oh, no one hired me." I asked what he was doing. He said, "I needed to work." He was on his way out the door. He simply wanted to thank me for allowing him to work. This was amazing. He wanted no money. I went out and caught up to him. "Let me at least feed you lunch." He didn't want it. I then asked him if he would join me for lunch. That he would do. This was a wonderful young man. He went the extra mile—in fact, he wasn't even asked to go the first mile.

He was busy at school. He had great parents and a scholarship. He didn't need money. He needed to work—to not be idle. The idle people standing by in this biblical story could have gone and worked.

Back to the story. When the day was over and it was pay time, the labourers who had worked all day were offended that the labourers who only worked an hour were paid the same.

You can read the Master's response. Remember, this scripture can only compare to the real marketplace to a certain extent. This is a parable; He starts the parable with, "For the kingdom of heaven is like..."

This part of his answer is fascinating, "Is it not lawful for me to do what I will with mine own? Is thine eye evil, because I am good?" (verse 15)

God is good and He will take care of us. There is not a certain amount of time we must work or tithes we must give to have Him love and reward us. We just need to show up at work, and leave the amount of reward up to Him.

Day 28: God's Day

Take this day and make it yours. Do it by doing God's will. Make this a memorable Sabbath.

Day 29: Don't Neglect Your Family

As we've said before: "God first, family second, work third." Involve your family in as many God-like activities as possible. Pray with them, talk with them—just be with them.

Day 30: Remember the Covenant

Read the words of the covenant once again. Remember God is true to His word. Study His words every day. They truly do point to eternal life. That is what is needed in our life: our actions, our thoughts, our desires they need to point to heaven.

There is plenty of sin around us. There is also so much that is beautiful, good, and noble. Think on great ideas, feast on great words, and then live a noble life.

Day 31: Love One Another

Look at Jesus's answer when He was questioned:

37 Jesus said unto him, Thou shalt love the Lord
thy God with all thy heart, and with all thy
soul, and with all thy mind.

38 This is the first and great commandment.

39 And the second is like unto it, thou shalt love
thy neighbor as thyself.

40 On these two commandments hang all the
law and the prophets.

Matthew 22:37-40

Our first allegiance is to God. His other concern is to obey
the commandments, but look at this next part: He doesn't
say to love our neighbors like a relative, or good friend, but
like ourselves.

In John, He gives a great comparison. He wants unity
among His disciples. I hope we are there in His number, even
though sinners we be. Read this and see how much He wants
us to love one another:

7 Now they have known that all things
whatsoever Thou hast given me are of thee.

8 For I have given unto them the words which
Thou gavest me; and they have received them,
and have known surely that I came out from
thee, and they have believed that Thou didst
send me.

9 I pray for them: I pray not for the world, but
for them which Thou hast given me; for they
are Thine.

10 And all mine are Thine, and Thine are mine;
and I am glorified in them.

11 And now I am no more in the world, but these
are in the world, and I come to Thee. Holy
Father, keep through Thine own name those
whom Thou hast given me, that they may be
one, as we are.

12 While I was with them in the world, I kept
them in Thy name: those that Thou gavest

me I have kept, and none of them is lost, but the Son of perdition; that the scripture might be fulfilled.

13 And now come I to Thee; and these things I speak in the world, that they might have my joy fulfilled in themselves.

14 I have given them Thy word; and the world hath hated them, because they are not of the world, even as I am not of the world.

15 I pray not that Thou shouldest take them out of the world, but that Thou shouldest keep them from the evil.

16 They are not of the world, even as I am not of the world.

17 Sanctify them through Thy truth: Thy word is truth.

18 As Thou hast sent me into the world, even so have I also sent them into the world.

19 And for their sakes I sanctify myself, that they also might be sanctified through the truth.

20 Neither pray I for these alone, but for them also which shall believe on me through their word;

21 That they all may be one; as Thou, Father, art in me, and I in Thee, that they also may be one in us: that the world may believe that Thou hast sent me.

22 And the glory which Thou gavest me I have given them; that they may be one, even as we are one:

23 I in them, and Thou in me, that they may be made perfect in one; and that the world may know that Thou hast sent me, and hast loved them, as Thou hast loved me.

24 Father, I will that they also, whom Thou hast given me, be with me where I am; that they may behold my glory, which Thou hast given me: for Thou lovedst me before the foundation of the world.

25 O righteous Father, the world hath not known Thee: but I have known thee, and these have known that Thou hast sent me.

26 And I have declared unto them Thy name, and will declare it: that the love wherewith Thou hast loved me may be in them, and I in them.

John 17:7-26

I'll close this section with Jesus's words. Read them again when you can pray and feel the spirit. Think of this prayer that Christ made to our Heavenly Father for us and on our behalf. I want to be a joint heir with this Jesus.

7 Beloved, let us love another: for love is of God; and every one that loveth is born of God and knoweth God.

8 He that loveth not knoweth not God; for God is love.

1 John 4:7-8

15

Blessed be the Lord God, the God of Israel, who only doeth wondrous things. And blessed be His glorious name for ever: and let the whole earth be filled with His glory; Amen, and Amen.
Psalm 72:18-19

What Do We Do Now?

I started composing this book about 10 years ago, but started compiling the final draft around 20 days ago. This time has been most enlightening and very rewarding. Let me share with you a few important things which have happened.

These principles are important to me. I try to earnestly live them. I hope God, my Maker, is pleased with how I've used His words. There was not one particular time that I felt I should write this book. It just is a natural part of where I am in my life and my career. One big desire I have is to not be phony about any of this. There is much more to write but I need to learn more before I can write more. I know a new set of experiences awaits me—and you.

I have loved every minute of this process. I can hardly sleep—I wake up early to read and write. I'm under the backboard playing basketball, getting knocked over because I'm thinking about this:

8   **This book of the law shall not depart out of thy mouth; but thou shalt meditate therein day and night, that thou mayest observe to do according to all that is written therein: for then thou shalt make thy way prosperous, and then thou shalt have good success.**

Joshua 1:8

Honestly, I've never been this intense about anything—
and I'm pretty intense. Often I feel like a section is not going well so it's back to the book or back on my knees. Then I
start to write what I think is important and five pages later I
realize that nothing of what is written is what I set out to
write. It is an amazing and humbling experience. Someone
out there must need this information.

I started with about four jam-packed pages of notes. I've
collected them for years. I'm done now and I have eight pages
of notes left over. Talk about the law of increase! Most of the
remaining scriptures and ideas have to do with various
strategies of success. So, you probably guessed it. I'm going
to write a new book. It will be called *Success Buy The Bible*.
I hope it will be useful. He can do more for us than we can
imagine:

> 20 **Now unto Him that is able to do exceeding
> abundantly above all that we ask or think,
> according to the power that worketh in us.**
>
> **Ephesians 3:20**

I want to leave you with a few parting ideas. Wealth is
delusional. Make no mistake about that. The adversary wants
us to miss God's mark. We need to energize our lives not to
be deceived. We should take no moral shortcuts. We can't
mortgage our future with the pleasures of today.

God will be true to His covenant. It is His and He said He
will be our God. If God is with us, who can be against us?
Never forget the Abrahamic Covenant, then maybe like Dives
we may make it to Abraham's bosom:

> 24 **And he cried and said, Father Abraham, have
> mercy on me, and send Lazarus, that he may
> dip the tip of his finger in water, and cool my
> tongue; for I am tormented in this flame.**
> 25 **But Abraham said, Son, remember that thou
> in thy lifetime receivedst thy good things, and
> likewise Lazarus evil things: but now he is
> comforted, and thou art tormented.**

26 And beside all this, between us and you there
is a great gulf fixed: so that they which would
pass from hence to you cannot; neither can
they pass to us, that would come from thence.

Luke 16:24-26

Wealth is fleeting. Wealth is what you have been given which enables you to serve others. As you've read this book, I hope you also realize that you must be a generous receiver. I have a lot. Still, people want to take me out to dinner or give me a nice gift. At first, I rejected their gifts. Another wise friend said, "How dare you! How dare you take away from them the blessing of giving?" Again, we are so interdependent. God loves a cheerful giver. We must also be a cheerful receiver.

I'd like to share with you a letter I received from a student of our stock market seminar. It is wonderfully written and very passionate:

Dear Wade:

I wish to thank you for your wonderful contributions. I'm writing not only to express my gratefulness, but to share an experience I had about two weeks ago that has more to do with the human experience than directly with financial success. On a Friday your tape arrived and I was wondering when I was going to find the time to listen to it. At 1:00 a.m. that very next morning there was an emergency call for me (I am a practicing vascular surgeon of 20 years). And I was groggily dreading another sleep-deprived weekend. On the way to the hospital, I heard most of the new tape, and was amazed at the transformation of how I felt. By now I was fully awake, alert, refreshed, and eagerly anticipating what lay in store.

I now realize what took place. You gave me something very important that early morning. That something is HOPE. Hope, one of our most powerful emotions, is the essence of motivation, and is priceless. Hope means different things to different people, but to me it means the promise of a less demanding professional life, of a life actually being with my family, of being able to retire from medicine rather than being retired by it, of financial security in essence. Hope is the future!

I profoundly thank you for rekindling that spirit that is within us all. Moreover, you are providing the power through which hope is operative. That power is EDUCATION, that engine we need to move us forward. Education is inestimable and irredeemable. You have that unique ability to make complex matters seem readily comprehensible. As a surgical educator I know what a rare gift this is. Again, I thank you for sharing your special talents.

Sincerely,

J.K., M.D.

I had to leave the office for awhile when I read this. I had no idea that what I was doing would have or could have such an impact on people. God has blessed me immensely. I hoped that His words were coming through in my actions. I've received letters and comments on my financial strategies, but not on hope. I was serendipity for Him. I have received countless blessings by trying to live a life guided by God's serendipity. You too, have had those times. I know it. I know of no one who has not had experiences that were unexpected joys, even life-changing events which lead them to the Master of Life.

Riches, in all this, are neutral. They are neither good nor bad. How we view them, what we will do for them and how we handle them once received is the concern. The problem is a problem of choice. What do we seek first?

We cannot limit God. Why would we want to try? We have enough to do. Matthew 12:35 says: "A good man out of the good treasure of the heart bringeth forth good things: and an evil man out of the evil treasure bringeth forth evil things." How did the treasure get into the heart? We have to feast on the words of God; make them real to us by doing His will. I don't have to tell you specific ways to riches. Follow God and they will come. Let's work hard to let His word abide in us.

John 15:7 says: "If ye abide in me, and my words abide in you, ye shall ask what ye will, and it shall be done unto you." What a fantastic statement!

16 Therefore it is of faith, that it might be by grace; to the end the promise might be sure to all the seed; not to that only which is of the law, but to that also which is of the faith of Abraham; who is the father of us all,

17 (As it is written, I have made thee a father of many nations,) before him whom he believed, even God, who quickeneth the dead, and calleth those things which be not as though they were.

18 Who against hope believed in hope, that he might become the father of many nations, according to that which was spoken, So shall thy seed be.

19 And being not weak in faith, he considered not his own body now dead, when he was about an hundred years old, neither yet the deadness of Sarah's womb:

20 He staggered not at the promise of God through unbelief; but was strong in faith, giving glory to God;

21 And being fully persuaded, that what He had promised, He was able also to perform.

22 And therefore it was imputed to him for righteousness.

23 Now it was not written for his sake alone, that it was imputed to him;

24 But for us also, to whom it shall be imputed, if we believe on Him that raised up Jesus our Lord from the dead;

25 Who was delivered for our offences, and was raised again for our justification.

Romans 4:16-25

9 Know therefore that the Lord thy God, He is God, the faithful God, which keepeth cove-

nant and mercy with them that love Him and keep His commandments to a thousand generations.

Deuteronomy 7:9

These two scriptures tie so well together: the new and the old. I offer the following Psalm for your edification:

1　Praise ye the Lord. Blessed is the man that feareth the Lord, that delighteth greatly in His commandments.
2　His seed shall be mighty upon earth: the generation of the upright shall be blessed.
3　Wealth and riches shall be in his house: and his righteousness endureth for ever.
4　Unto the upright there ariseth light in the darkness: he is gracious, and full of compassion, and righteous.
5　A good man sheweth favour, and lendeth: he will guide his affairs with discretion.
6　Surely he shall not be moved for ever: the righteous shall be in everlasting remembrance.
7　He shall not be afraid of evil tidings: his heart is fixed, trusting in the Lord.
8　His heart is established, he shall not be afraid, until he see his desire upon his enemies.
9　He hath dispersed, he hath given to the poor; his righteousness endureth for ever; his horn shall be exalted with honour.

Psalm 112:1-9

Let's get on with it. There's a life to live, much to receive, and much to give!

Appendix

A

Scriptures Used

Following is a list of all scriptures used in this book.

Proverbs

James

II Peter

I John

III John

Revelation

Appendix

B

Paying Your Mortgage

Don't think that you've heard this before. There are simple ways to pay off any debt faster. This will deal with your home mortgage. If you want to be debt-free, then read and apply the following principle.

As you can tell, the next page shows an amortization schedule on a $140,000 mortgage at an 8.75% interest rate and a monthly payment (principal and interest) of $1,200. Taxes and insurance are extra.

When you make your payment (Line 1) of $1,200, $1,020.83 is going to interest. Yes, it is currently tax deductible, but it is still huge. Only $179.17 is going off of the principal balance. Do you know if at the same time you sent in $180.48, or the principal for payment on Line 2, that over the course of the loan, you would save $1,019.52 in interest? That's right—save that huge chunk of interest. Your new balance will be $139,640.35 (Line 3)

Think of this. A small extra principal payment now saves so much. You can even pay several extra principal payments. Again, if when you send in the $1,200 and were to add a separate check for $180.48 (Line 2), $181.79 (Line 3), and

Amortization Payment Schedule

Line	Balance	Payment	Interest (8.75%)	Principal	New Balance
1	$140,000.00	$1,200	$1,020.83	$179.17	$139,820.83
2	$139,820.83	$1,200	$1,019.52	$180.48	$139,640.35
3	$139,640.35	$1,200	$1,018.21	$181.79	$139,458.56
4	$139,458.56	$1,200	$1,016.88	$183.12	$139,275.44
5	$139,275.44	$1,200	$1,015.55	$184.45	$139,090.99
6	$139,090.99	$1,200	$1,014.21	$185.79	$138,905.20
7	$138,905.20	$1,200	$1,012.85	$187.15	$138,718.05

$183.12 (Line 4), or a total of $545.39, you would save $1,019.52, $1,018.21, and $1,016.88, or $3,054.61 in interest payments. Your new balance will be $139,275.44.

Look at how fast it pays down through these miscellaneous points:

- Later on when the principal payment is larger than the interest payment you may not be able to do this, but now at the beginning the extra principal payment is probably affordable, and a payment now means the greatest interest savings.

- You can get a 30-year mortgage (smaller payments than a 15-year mortgage) and make these extra payments on your own. Think of this. If you make one extra principal payment you will pay off a 30-year mortgage in 15 years. If you make two extra (that's the main payment, plus two extra principal payments) you will pay it off in 10 years. If you make three extra payments, it will pay off in 7-1/2 years. Four will pay off the 30-year mortgage in six years. Just divide 30 by the number of principal payments to get this number.

- You still have to pay the full next month's payment. If you paid the $1,200 plus the $545.39, you still owe a minimum of $1,200 next month.

- I've never seen this type of pay down ever affect or trigger prepayment penalties. These extra payments just don't add up fast enough to affect such a penalty.

- Be explicit with your instructions to the bank on what to do with the extra money. Don't take this lightly. Tell them you want the extra principal payment to apply either to the "extra principal payments" section, or to the loan balance. If you don't they might put the money in the escrow or impounds section (and hold with no interest for property taxes and insurance payments). No kidding. I even send a separate check with a letter and they (the bank) still mess it up. Double check to make sure the principal was posted correctly.

- You can pay any amount you want. Instead of the $545.39, you could pay $600. The only point is that you're off the preprinted schedule! With $29 amortization programs available, you can do your own new schedule, but if you want to stay on the bank's schedule then add up the payments and pay to the penny.

Virtually everyone in my real estate seminars got this except math majors. They just don't understand amortizing loans, well at least a few haven't.

Remember, you save the most at the beginning of a loan and that is when it costs so little to save so much. Use this strategy with the multiple returns you'll receive by following other principles in this book and you'll soon be debt free.

Appendix

C

Tax Structuring

You have no doubt heard of estate planning and financial planning. That is the old way of looking at your financial life. What I do and what I teach is entity planning—actually using different entities to structure your affairs, thereby reducing your taxes, lessening exposure to risks and liabilities, preparing for a great retirement, and then making sure your family or church receives everything you've worked so hard to build up. The following is given here to help you structure your affairs wisely.

Entity structuring is quite simple, yet the ramifications of wise entity structuring are quite dynamic and far-reaching. The results are not only a diversity of investments and business interests, but also a diversity of entities owning or controlling those same investments. Let's preview each possible entity:

Corporation
The backbone of your family liability protection—a workhorse that adds so much to all the other entities.
1) It is perpetual—it does not end.
2) Different classes of stock can be issued.
3) Different voting rights can be applied to different shares.

4) The officers are protected.
5) Shareholders have no personal liability.
6) It has incredible tax advantages:
   a) Works with a pension plan.
   b) Can have fiscal year end different from Dec. 31.
   c) Can make forgivable loan.
   d) Can institute an asset freeze.
   e) Can have deductible investments.
   f) Operates multiple businesses.
   g) Can be established in Nevada to take advantage of laws: privacy, taxes, et cetera. Call Wade Cook Seminars, Inc. for a free cassette seminar on the power of Nevada Corporation. 1-800-872-7411.
   h) Can deduct travel for business—for attending meetings, and too many numerousexpenses to mention here.
   i) Can be "S" or "C" corporation and receive tax benefits.
7) It protects assets.
8) It is an estate planning tool: dividing up stock, defering taxes, setting up a trust control, et cetera.
9) It can own stock in other corporations or units in Limited Partnerships.

Living Trust
The umbrella entity.
1) Helps avoid probate—saves time, money, exposure.
2) Provides some estate planning.
3) Saves on estate taxes.
4) Allows for stepped-up basis to avoid capital gains taxes while one spouse is living.
5) Provides for smooth transition of business enterprise.
6) Allows you to provide for children and grandchildren or charities.

Pension Plan
Work hard—retire rich. Create a tax-free entity.
1) Provides a tax haven.
2) Like a forced savings plan.

3) Donations are tax deductible.
4) Investments grow tax-free until distributed.
5) Safety is unsurpassed.
6) Borrowing money allowed for certain items.
7) Combination of plans allows for maximum contribution—up to $30,000 in defined contribution plans.
8) "Self-Trusteed"—you control everything.
9) All income (dividend, investment, interest) is received tax free.

Business Trust
The best for leasing business equipment.
1) Establishes separate entity for security.
2) Operates independently of other entities.
3) Set up as a leasing company to lease or rent equipment back to your other companies.

Limited Partnership
A different entity for different purposes.
1) Good for families with large asset base.
2) Several at one time can control separate investments.
3) Works nicely with the corporate structure.
4) Allows maximum and effective use of the gift giving rules.
5) Difficult for creditors to get at assets.
6) Integral part of APT (Asset Protection Trust), an off-shore entity providing fantastic protection.
7) Offers superior methods for distributing income to children for tax savings (unearned income).
8) Can own stock in corporations or units in other partnerships.
9) Can be used in conjunction with corporation for maximum tax benefits (Corporation as General Partner).
10) Distribution is considered "unearned income" and is not subject to social security taxes.

Charitable Remainder Trust

Deductions and many benefits later. Note: If you go to church and want the church, or its schools, or any of its programs to receive all or part of your wealth, then this entity is invaluable. It allows you to pay a large final "tithe" on your life's work.

1) Used for tax planning now and donations of certain investments to charity.
2) Special rule allows for "Pension Type" aspect—draws out substantial income later.
3) Protects family interests.
4) Lessens (maybe eliminates) your "taxable estate" and saves money.

Most of you need three or four of these different entities. They work together, not alone. The audio seminars in my

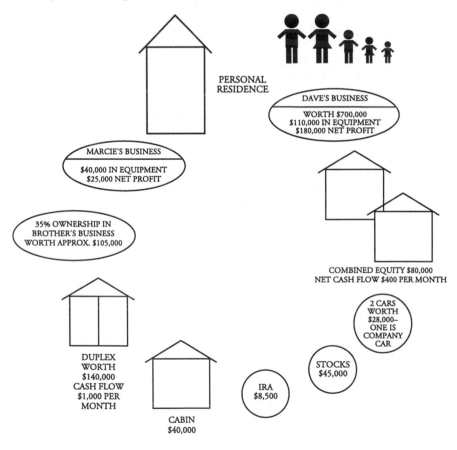

Financial Fortress course will teach you how to integrate and use the various entities.

Because of the nature or function of each particular entity, they work with each other. I'll give one typical example here:

An Integration of Entities

Let's look at entity structuring for the Lincoln family: Dave, Marcie, and their three children. Dave has a manufacturing company, which is growing quite rapidly and takes a lot of his time. It's worth about $700,000, owns about $110,000 worth of equipment, and produced about $180,000 in net profits this year. However, it is a high-risk business and he is constantly worried about lawsuits.

Marcie has a typesetting business. She works part-time and has one other part-time employee. Her business is a sole proprietorship with $40,000 worth of equipment. She nets about $25,000 a year.

Their home is worth $280,000 with an $80,000 mortgage. They have no formal retirement plan, but do have $8,500 in IRAs. They own a cabin in the mountains worth $40,000. They have stock investments of $45,000 in their personal name. They have a duplex (free and clear) worth $140,000 and two other rental houses with combined equities of $80,000.

Dave's brother has a software company worth $300,000. Dave's share is 35% or $105,000 because he put up $40,000 to help found the business. He draws no money now but expects some in a few years.

This year the Lincolns will pay about $45,000 in taxes. You can see they:

1) **Have no serious lawsuit protection strategies (only liability insurance).**
    a) One lawsuit could ruin everything.
    b) Liability for the brother's debts is possible.

2) Have no serious tax planning vehicles.
   a) Some into IRA.
   b) Sole proprietorship.
      1) No diversion of funds—year end, etc.
      2) No corporate brackets.
      3) All income to one bracket.
      4) Could use CRT.

3) Have no estate planning vehicles.
   a) No stock splitting.
   b) No asset freeze.
   c) No Living Trust.

4) Have no serious pension planning.
   a) No Keogh or, better yet, corporate pension plan.
   b) No tax deductions.
   c) No tax-free growth.
   d) No control.

If you are seeing an analysis like this for the first time, don't let it confuse you. Stick with it and you'll see the logic behind each move. Also, don't expect your CPA or financial planner to understand this. They're locked into their old, ineffective strategies. It will take you a half hour, maybe one full hour, to grasp all the ramifications of integrating entities. But it will take them weeks because they have to undo so much wrong information that's been fed into their brains for 20 years.

Remember, we're not here for quick fixes or bandaids. We are taking a "holistic" approach to complete wealth enhancement, entity integration, tax strategies, retirement planning and estate structuring. You'll take an integral role in setting this up.

I once met a couple with 12 children. I asked them how they kept track of all their names. They looked at me like I was crazy. They rattled them off so fast I barely caught one. Likewise, this will be your family of entities. You know them by what they do, by their functions. You can have nicknames

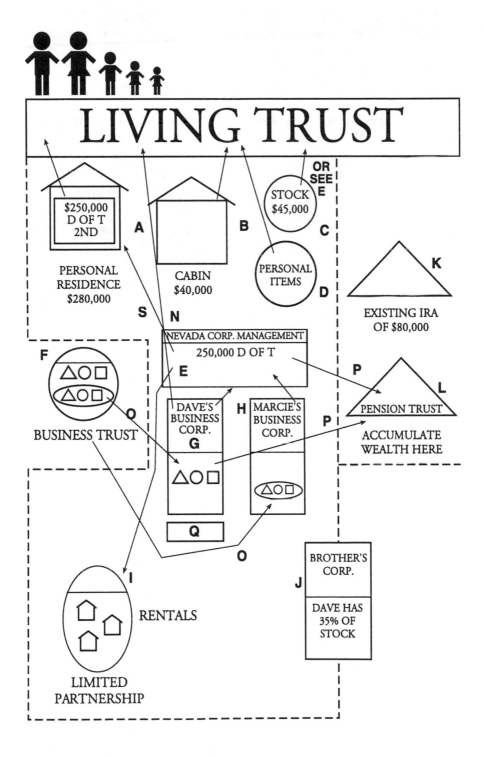

LIVING TRUST

$250,000
D OF T
2ND

PERSONAL
RESIDENCE
$280,000

A

CABIN
$40,000

B

STOCK
$45,000

OR
SEE
E

C

PERSONAL
ITEMS

D

K

EXISTING IRA
OF $80,000

S

N

NEVADA CORP. MANAGEMENT
250,000 D OF T

E

F

BUSINESS TRUST

O

DAVE'S
BUSINESS
CORP.
G

H

MARCIE'S
BUSINESS
CORP.

P

P

PENSION TRUST

L

ACCUMULATE
WEALTH HERE

Q

O

I

RENTALS

LIMITED
PARTNERSHIP

J

BROTHER'S
CORP.

DAVE HAS
35% OF
STOCK

for each entity, like TOP for Technical Optional Products, Inc. You'll love seeing your growth, keeping tax money working for you and retirement accounts building—all protected and ready to meet any contingency.

1) **Your personal residence should be assigned to your Living Trust.**
   a) Unless you're really susceptible to lawsuits (then perhaps a Family Limited Partnership is better).
   b) Residence goes to stepped up basis if one spouse dies and the other spouse sells property. But that's not all; all property, stock, units, rentals, or other investments go to stepped up basis if owned in Living Trust.
   c) Equity should be encumbered. See "N."

2) **Cabin—Put in Living Trust.**

3) **Stocks—Put in Living Trust.**
   a) Assign either individual stocks or whole brokerage account to Living Trust.
   b) Possibly divvy up to other corporations.
      1) Trade stock—public for private.
      2) If dividends are taken—take advantage of 70% exclusion rule.

4) **Personal Items—Assign to Schedule A of Living Trust.**

5) **Management Corporation—Nevada.**
   a) Move money—deduct—to "no tax" state.
   b) Could own property, but should not own too much. This is a "cash flow" entity.
   c) Manage other corporations—by contract.
   d) General partner for Limited Partnership.
   e) Put lien on personal residence to encumber equity.
   f) If you do #5, try to make name like a bank, (Capital Funding Corporation).
   g) Put money into corporate pension plan.

6) **Business Trust—Equipment Leasing.**
   a) Buy, hold, lease equipment to corporation.
   b) Corporations lease or rent.
   c) Use proper forms—UCC, etc.

7) **Big Corporation.**
   a) Divvy up stock to children or others.
   b) Do asset freeze on parent's preferred stock.
   c) Pay management company—Nevada.
   d) Pay leasing company for equipment.
   e) Don't own equipment.
   f) Consider even putting land (building) in separate Limited Partnership.
   g) Try to establish as many "independent contractors" as possible instead of employees.
   h) Pay money to pension fund (or see E-7).

8) **Corporation (Nevada)—Typesetting.**
   a) Avoid personal liability.
   b) Tax structure—fiscal year end, asset freeze, lower brackets.
   c) Lease equipment from business trust.
   d) Pay money to management corporation (or keep, if lower bracket).
   e) Possibly have own pension fund.

9) **Limited Partnership.**
   a) Own existing rentals.
   b) Let corporation be general partner—avoid personal liability.
   c) Initially issue all assets to Dave and Marcie (Living Trust Schedule A).
   d) Gift units ($10,000 worth per year) to each child, or hold in trust for them.

10) **Brother's Business.**
    a) Should be corporation for all the above reasons. Dave and Marcie avoid liability.

b) Dave's percentage of ownership assigned to other entities—Living Trust is a good bet. Could be assigned to other corporations or directly to children.

11) IRA.
a) Keep separate.
b) Review beneficiary payout (see if different combinations work).
c) Keep adding more.

12) Pension Account.
a) Set up and contribute as much as possible.
b) Include employer—consider 401K: Corporation G.
c) Take aggressive stance with money in plan—later, as current business demands so much.
d) Get investment with high growth-diversify later.

13) Management Corporation to be general partner of Family Limited Partnership.

14) Lien.
a) Dave and Marcie have too much equity-a big target.
b) Trade stock for a mortgage. Record it so there is no equity available.
c) All home owners should "homestead" their houses to protect equity.

15) Business Trust leases equipment to Corporation.
a) It earns money.
b) Pay money to children to avoid dividend (double taxation) treatment.

16) Pay (contribute) money to pension funds.
Fully deductible—great tax savings.

17) Own land, but keep building as separate entity—Corporation leases building from Partnership.

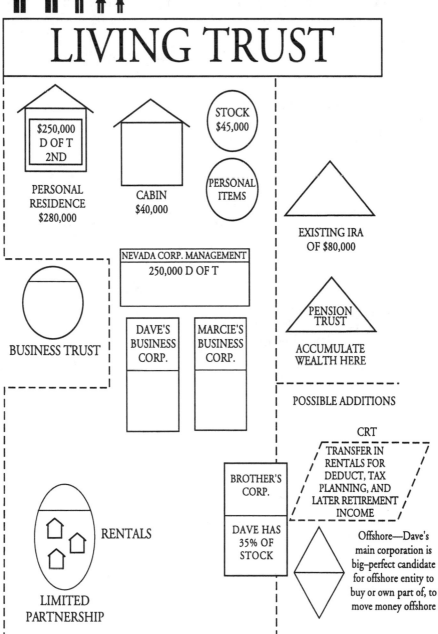

LIVING TRUST

$250,000 D OF T 2ND

PERSONAL RESIDENCE $280,000

CABIN $40,000

STOCK $45,000

PERSONAL ITEMS

EXISTING IRA OF $80,000

NEVADA CORP. MANAGEMENT
250,000 D OF T

BUSINESS TRUST

DAVE'S BUSINESS CORP.

MARCIE'S BUSINESS CORP.

PENSION TRUST

ACCUMULATE WEALTH HERE

POSSIBLE ADDITIONS

CRT

BROTHER'S CORP.

DAVE HAS 35% OF STOCK

TRANSFER IN RENTALS FOR DEDUCT, TAX PLANNING, AND LATER RETIREMENT INCOME

RENTALS

LIMITED PARTNERSHIP

Offshore—Dave's main corporation is big–perfect candidate for offshore entity to buy or own part of, to move money offshore

Note that if the corporation folds, the building is still controlled—the equipment is owned by a business trust. The corporation has cash flow, but no substantial assets.

Because of the net profits and value of the entities (business assets), Dave and Marcie are strong candidates for an Offshore Entity or Charitable Remainder Trust. Now review the previous diagram. Note that trusts cannot be put inside trusts.

- Pension Trust
- Business Trust
- CRT
- Offshore Trust

Also, just because we have a corporation drawn inside the trust does not mean it controls the corporation. In reality, Dave's and Marcie's stock holdings are the items owned by the trust.

These entities are designed to let you put God first, your family second, and your business third. If you really want to do more for your church in the way of huge donations, then check out my "Retirement Prosperity" Home Study Course. I look forward to meeting you at one of my seminars!

Appendix

D

What People Say

Following are a few of the letters received by Wade Cook Seminars, Inc. and Lighthouse Publishing Group, Inc. over the last few months. They are included to show you how Wade Cook and his company are helping people every day.

Ed

Recently, a good friend got laid off. I was able to help him. I've been helping a lot of my friends and my son get involved in trading the Wade Cook way. It's been very rewarding to me to be in this position. I'm retired. In the last three months I netted more than I grossed in a year as an airline pilot for a major international airline. 25 years of a major airline flying wide-body international at $175,000 a year. I have netted more money writing covered calls. I'm helping and training my friends, providing an opportunity for them. I'm in Florida, so when the market opens at 9:30, I can do my trades, go play a round of golf, come home, and do some more trades, and it's wonderful. I couldn't have done it otherwise, trust me. I've tried futures and trading and stuff. I've found a nice niche with the covered calls and I stay within the rules you have taught and it's very risk-free. Thank you for teaching me to do this.

Betty

I was looking for a way to make money from my home that was fun, not the every day job. I've found it, thanks to Wade. I can see my kids at 8:00, send them off to school, the market opens at 8:30, it closes at 3:30, the kids come home and my work day is through. I can be here for my family and still help with little things.

Lisa

The Wall Street Workshop enabled me to live my financial dream. I have enough income from doing the stock trades that I'm not going to the office every day. I can stay at home and do my stock trades. Life's too short to be stuck in a 9:00 to 5:00. I started off doing temporary work, doing secretarial for Boeing, some other major corporations in the northwest, and I love to paint, I love to do sculpture and I was afraid to do that because I didn't want to be a starving artist. I like my comfort. Doing the stock market trades has allowed me to quit working 9:00 to 5:00, to go out and make money, and have the confidence to stay home and do what I want to do.

Ed

I have been to the Wall Street Workshop, listened to the **Zero to Zillions** tapes, and read Wade's book. I am doing some covered calls right now with returns around 15% to 20% per month. I have over $300,000 in my stock portfolio and would like to leverage this money to retire my wife from her job so she can be a full-time mom and also to help our church retire its debt. Thanks for your help.

J.J.

Mr. Cook, you have done a great service in preparing the information, developing the courses, sharing with others the methods you have developed just being in the marketplace. Your tapes, video and text material is invaluable. Your most important lesson is a spiritual one, and that is to develop the habit to give back to God. These are important messages and habits to develop to strengthen family values. God bless you.

Linn

This seminar has helped me in moving on to the next step in my financial development. The course was all that I hoped it would be. It caused me to make my first trades. On the second day of the class I made two covered call plays and made $1875.00! This was a total return of more than 20%. It was great.

Rick

I'm writing this to express my thanks on teaching us Wade Cook's strategies for success in the stock market.

My brother, friend, and I have been trading for two years with very little success. In fact, we were getting so discouraged and short of funds that we were almost ready to give up . . ..After reading "Stock Market Miracles," we called your number and had some tapes sent to us. All three of us listened to those tapes, completely fascinated. We decided we would either learn to do this using Mr. Cook's strategies or we would not trade anymore. All three of us attended your workshop.

During the workshop we made $234 on a quick option trade. Since the weekend, about a month and a half now, we made about $1200 on covered calls. On April 30th, we hit our first homerun. Using the strategy of trading options on an announcement we purchased options on a company at a 68¢ premium and in three days we sold the option at 3 1/8. We had a profit of over $11,000. Even our broker was amazed.

Because of Mr. Cook and your organization, we now have a new lease on our trading.

Frank

You'll never know how much you have done for me and my family. I'm new to all of this. I opened a trading account and IRA on April 14 at Dean Witter. As part of preparation for this workshop. I did my first trade on April 21. As of May 1 I am $1,100 ahead on a $4,500 initial account. That's $1,100 in 10 days! Nearly 25% in 10 days!

Debra

We started investing, using Wade's strategies, on April Fool's Day 1997. As of April 30, 1997, our $10,000 account opened with a liquidation balance of $16,945! This is exciting! We had done options, covered calls, some stock purchases and some puts. We hope to be *free* as soon as possible!

John

As a stockbroker, I can say that this is the most valuable wokshop that I have attended. While I have learned the mechanics of investing, this is the first real opportunity that I have had to learn the *strategies* of investing. I cannot wait to attend the other workshops, and also to bring close friends and family to future workshops. Wade Cook has one devoted disciple in me!

Bryan

Now I feel that I have found my destiny, *MAKING MONEY*! My father is a well-known preacher, and I have been the rebellious kid in the past. As I started to become more involved in the market I shared with my dad the returns I was making on the money my granddad gave me and my cousin to invest. After he saw what I made him in the first two months he was constantly encouraging me to stay at it. He tells all of his other pastor friends what I have done for him and now I have hundreds of thousands of dollars.

Wade, I must tell you that you have taken me from the dumps to a millionare over night, and a billionaire in 5-7 years. All of those countless seminars I went to have paid off. I very much enjoyed your staff and their professionalism. I have been to so many of your seminars that they know me well.

To all who read this I must tell you that Wade Cook is for real. He is more than just a teaching money machine, he is a man with Biblical conviction and morals. And his services like WIN and WIN Plus are outstanding.

Ken and Pam

I just want to thank you for being the vehicle that has changed my life. I have tried several money making ideas over the years and this is the first that produced results as claimed and has kept my interest.

Stewart

My wife and I attended the Seattle Wall Street Workshop the first of March and it was awesome ....I started this year with $5,000 in a Smith Barney account and in spite of the bad months of February and March, I have just about doubled my money working at it part time. I have no doubt that these strategies work and I am so thankful I had the radio on one morning and heard your message.

Chuck

I figured the small investment for your book *Wall Street Money Machine* would be worth the risk. I was so impressed that I subscribed to the WIN bulletin board. Now my life has changed forever!

An example of one of my first investments was in Sybase Inc. (SYBS). I purchased 300 shares on October 2, 1996, and then sold three covered call contracts on them and was called out October 18, 1996. My return was 23.73% in 16 days or a 534% annualized return.

Wade you are a godsend. Thank you for providing the tools and information to really make money and have more time for church and family.

Robert

I want to thank you for exposing me to such an exciting way to make money. I've had a $21,000 day and a $23,900 day (after commission). I average about $3,000 a day. My family and friends have shared in this knowledge and are also very appreciative. I can't thank you enough. At my age the adrenaline is really flowing again, God bless you.

Jim

You have shown me how to generate my retirement income. In the last half of this year, I generated $70,000.

Wendy

This is a blessing to our family and an answer to our prayers. It is going to make the difference between night and day to our finances. It is going to make our families' future brighter than I dreamed. And I know enough about stocks to know everyone at this workshop is so lucky to have the opportunity to learn this information. Without knowing very much about dividend capturing before this workshop, we made over $1,700 in a few days on an irregular dividend!

Joni

We are now even much more financially positioned for early retirement and to contribute more to charity. If someone calls for a donation I feel like I can help—and what a good and rewarding feeling it is. To help someone who is in need get ahead is our challenge, and gives great purpose in our lives.

The seminar also has brought our whole family together. My husband and I now share many thoughts and discussions about stock trades, future picks, et cetera—and having fun doing it! I talk to my mom on the phone at least three times a day. She is 65 and can finally financially afford to build her lifetime dream home! (she has for the last 25 years lived in a single-wide mobile home on a dairy farm and has worked hard her whole life to build her own home and now it is possible with her wise investments and your Wade Cook strategies! Thank you!) My two brothers are also being successful with your strategies, every time we meet we share ideas and investment tips. Again, what *fun*!

We hope these dreams will become possible for other people who have the drive to seek opportunities and make things happen.

Robyn

I want to thank you so much for the knowledge I obtained from your Wall Street Workshop. It enabled me to retire from work at 42 years of age. I am a mother of 4-year old and 20-month old sons. During my retirement I have been able to spend so much more precious time with them that I otherwise would not (they spent about 9-10 hours per day in day care before). We sometimes go to the playground, shopping (now that I have more money we can buy what we want to!), or just hang out at home.

I'm not making millions yet but plan to attend the Next Step seminar to speed up my profit-making career. My husband is now anxious to be able to retire, so I'm working on that now. Even in the flat market I'm able to make enough on covered calls to live on. Our future goals are to take the kids out of day care completely, move to the West Coast, build a new home near the San Juan Islands, in Washington, and live our dreams.

You'll never know how much you have done for me and my family.

Douglas

On April 9, 1997, I started trading on behalf of a Foreign Corporation with $37,000. As of April 22, 1997, 10 days later, I have received cash in account of $16,739.67 (this is net—minus commissions). That's a 45% return in 10 days. Annualizing it out, it becomes 1,620%. But that's not the good news.

What this has allowed me to do is spend more time working our charitable foundation. I work about one hour in the morning on the stock market, one hour at lunch and then one hour at night preparing for the next day. (The foundation was set up to make grants to organizations that facilitate Judeo-Christian values especially as relating towards families.)

I praise the Lord for the education that we received from Wade Cook's organization (especially Paul Cook) and I cannot believe that we have done 54 trades and have only lost on one so far.

Thank you for the knowledge.

Ken and Pam

I especially appreciate your references to the Bible. I believe that it is the number one book to live your life by. If every home had a Bible that was read and a copy of the Wall Street Workshop, this would be a better world.

Thank you again, Wade, for helping me give more money to my Lord and helping me realize my goal of being a helping hand to people less fortunate.

Paul

I am now making a living trading stocks and options. This has been a wonderful change in my life, both for myself and my family.

Chris and Paul

This has been a life-changing experience. It is not often you see milestones occurring in life right before your eyes. In five days we have shielded our assets as well as earned over 50% of our initial investment. We are confident that we will be able to do this again and again.

Maria

I was very pleased to learn the strategies taught in the seminar. I have been investing in mutual funds and I thought I was doing well, but learning this I'm ready to change gears and make some real money so I can work when I want and spend more time with my family. I'm very excited! Thank you.

Brian

I've dreamed of being able to write one of these letters. Where do I start but to say that I attended the March 9-11 Wall Street Workshop in Santa Barbara. This is my second workshop. The first time I didn't follow through, but before attending this seminar I decided to just follow directions and "follow the formulas"—period.

I started my account with $2,000 the day before the seminar and made two trades before noon. I did not put in additional money until March 24, and now have a total of $12,450 invested. I've made a total of five covered call plays and two options plays, and have already made $5,100 (over 40%) and the month is not even out. I will make two additional plays before the month's expiration date. If I get called out on the stocks that I should, I will be over a 50% profit in one month. The amazing thing, is that this last week the stock market has gone down more than any other week in years and I still make money!

I'm excited and will share this with others. I'm already going to sponsor some others to the next local Wall Street Workshop. This is going to change my life. Thanks for sharing all the information you have learned. I only hope I can change other lives as your class has changed mine with the knowledge I now have.

---

*For more information on attending
the Wall Street Workshop, call 1-800-872-7411,
or for a complete product catalogue,
call the Lighthouse Publishing Group, Inc.
at 1-800-706-3547.*